The
Great Unknown
of the
Rio Grande

Books by Louis F. Aulbach

Buffalo Bayou, An Echo of Houston's Wilderness Beginnings
*Camp Logan (*with Linda Gorski and Robbie Morin*)*
The Devils River
The Fresno Rim
The Great Unknown of the Rio Grande
*The Lower Canyons of the Rio Grande (*with Joe Butler*)*
*The Lower Pecos River (*with Jack Richardson*)*
*The Upper Canyons of the Rio Grande (*with Linda Gorski*)*

The
Great Unknown
of the
Rio Grande

Terlingua Creek to La Linda

Including Boquillas Canyon and Mariscal Canyon

Second Edition

by

Louis F. Aulbach

Louis F. Aulbach, Publisher
Houston, Texas
2014

This guide has been compiled as an aid to canoeists. However, rivers change with time. We have tried to present a fair and accurate evaluation of the river and the conditions of the environment. Suggestions made in this guide can be invalidated by water and weather conditions, the skill of your paddling party, and changes in the river itself. We therefore cannot take responsibility for errors or omissions, or for problems encountered through the use of this guide. YOU are responsible for your own safety on the river. Use common sense and good judgment.

For Rachel, Laurence and Luther, Stephen, and Matthew and Amanda

Preface

One of the pleasures found in writing a guidebook such as this is that one generally does not do the ground work alone. Canoeing, especially wilderness expedition canoeing, is a social adventure. Several people have accompanied me on the trips through these sections of the Rio Grande over the years. A number of them have taken photos along the way, and I have been able to use a few of the fine pictures taken on our trips in this book. Others have joined me in exploratory trips into the backcountry of Big Bend National Park on seemingly futile searches for the ruins of the many archeological and historical sites that dot the land along the river. Some of those explorations have been the most enjoyable times in the research of this book because of the profound sense of discovery.

I would especially like to thank Dana Enos for his willingness to join each exploration at a moment's notice whether it entailed an extended journey on the river or a day hike into the barren desert. Dana also helped me with the more mundane research in the Archives of the Big Bend and the resources of the Center for Big Bend Studies at Sul Ross University. Linda Gorski also spent a lot of time with us walking the desert to the ruins along the river, and she made a special contribution to the research and to the promotion of the book. Terry Burgess is one who brought his camera on our trips and he has provided a number of fine photos that I hope tell more of the story than my written words. Fraser and Janice Baker made the final trip through Boquillas Canyon a special adventure, and Fraser has contributed some significant photographic records of the events. Many thanks, as well, go to Natalie Wiest, John Rich, John and Anne Olden, and all of the others whom I have forgotten to mention (and I do apologize) who contributed in their own way to the completion of this book.

Louis F. Aulbach

Houston, Texas
August, 2006

A Note on Footnotes

There are footnotes placed in the text throughout this book. These footnotes refer to the numeric list of Footnotes and Bibliographic References on page 97. The bibliographic reference is the source of the information indicated by the footnote.

Location Map

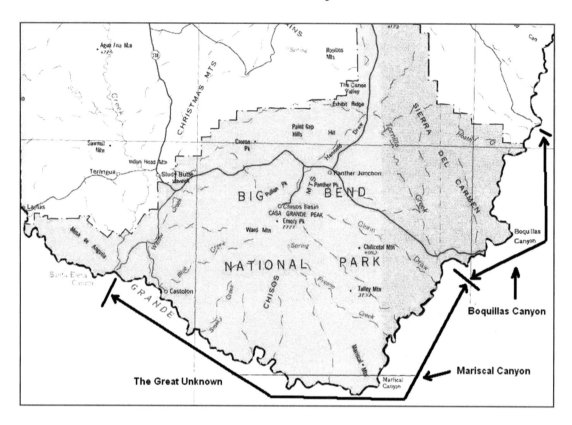

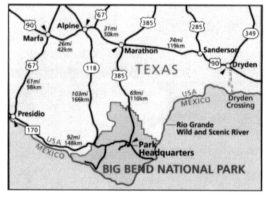

The Great Unknown of the Rio Grande, including Mariscal and Boquillas Canyons, is located in the Big Bend National Park, Texas.

The Big Bend National Park is at the southernmost end of the large bend made by the Rio Grande in its southeasterly course to the Gulf of Mexico. This vast and remote region is a long way from just about everywhere. The nearest large cities are El Paso, 329 miles to the west, and San Antonio, 406 miles to the east.

From El Paso on the west or from San Antonio on the east, take U. S. Highway 90 to either Alpine or Marathon. Take State Highway 118 about 76 miles south from Alpine to the west entrance to the park. From Marathon, take U. S. Highway 385 about 39 miles south to the north entrance to the park.

Table of Contents

Introduction

This is a guide for canoeing, kayaking or rafting the section of the Rio Grande in Big Bend National Park beginning at Terlingua Creek, the exit point for Santa Elena Canyon, and ending at the bridge at La Linda, the starting point for trips through the Lower Canyons. There are actually two distinct river trips described in this guide. The larger segment is the Great Unknown of the Rio Grande, and the smaller segment is a trip through the popular Boquillas Canyon. A shorter trip in the Great Unknown is often made through Mariscal Canyon.

Although this river segment is called the Great Unknown, the land along the Rio Grande in Big Bend National Park has been "known" quite well since the late nineteenth century. A wide range of agricultural and industrial pursuits have taken place in the Big Bend in the past one hundred twenty years, and a relatively large population of farmers, miners and ranchers have called the area their home.

It is only to the modern visitor to the park that the stories of the lives of the inhabitants of the area are unknown. In fact, so much of the history of the region has yet to be fully told that the story of this part of the Rio Grande is a great unknown. In addition to being a guide to the river, this book also attempts to reveal some of the history of the people who lived here and the events that occurred here, in the hope that a better awareness will encourage you to take the time to research the people, places and events of the Big Bend further.

It should also be noted that although this is a river guide, the fact that the river road follows the river from Terlingua Creek to Boquillas Canyon opens this area to one who is not floating the river. The road permits many of the scenes and sites to be seen by motor vehicle instead of water craft. And, to be honest, there are some places which are totally impractical to visit from the river. But, of course, the best can only be seen from the river.

The Great Unknown and Boquillas Canyon river trips are paddling adventures through a remote and rugged desert wilderness environment. Although these trips contain somewhat less technically challenging river conditions than adjacent sections of the Upper Canyons and the Lower Canyons, they do involve moving water and inaccessible locations where all appropriate preparations and precautions should be taken to ensure the safety of your group. Conditions on the river can change as quickly as the weather, and hazardous situations may present themselves at short notice.

The Shuttle

The planning for any trip includes the shuttle. The distances between the put in and the take out make it convenient to have your vehicles at the take out. The shuttles for the Great Unknown and for Boquillas Canyon are fairly long. However, they do have the advantage of being on paved roads that do not require high clearance vehicles.

The Mariscal Canyon "day trip" requires driving to the put in and the take out via the unpaved River Road. River Road is usually open to high clearance vehicles, but at times, it may require a four wheel drive vehicle. Be sure to confirm the road conditions prior to your departure.

Several shuttle services are available in the Big Bend for the Great Unknown, Boquillas Canyon and Mariscal Canyon trips. The cost of the shuttle service varies widely depending on how you arrange your specific service. Call or write the shuttle service well in advance of your trip for pricing and reservations. Those whom we have used and have found to be reliable are:

Big Bend River Tours
800-545-4240
432-371-3033
http://www.bigbendrivertours.com

Desert Sports
432-371-2727
888-989-6900
http://www.desertsportstx.com

Far Flung Outdoor Center
800-839-7238
http://bigbendfarflung.com

Ted Thayer
Highway 90 West
P. O. Box 402
Marathon, TX 79842
432-386-2928

Secure parking is available at Rio Grande Village and at Heath Canyon Ranch (at La Linda). Secure parking and access to the river is provided at the Heath Canyon Ranch for a small fee. Call Fred at 480-755-5755 for information and reservations.

The Permit

Effective February 1, 2007, a backcountry and river use fee of $10.00 per permit is required of all persons floating the Rio Grande in Big Bend National Park. This section of the river has been designated a part of the United States Wild and Scenic River System and is administered by the National Park Service in the Big Bend National Park. Call the ranger station at Panther Junction (915-477-2251) for the current river levels, river information, and permit requirements. Check the Wild & Scenic River web site at: **http://www.nps.gov/RIGR/index.htm** for the latest information. River levels are available on the International

Boundary and Water Commission web site: **http://www.ibwc.state.gov/home.html/**

The sections of the "General Regulations of River Use" that apply to the Great Unknown are summarized in a section at the back of this book. Do not hesitate to confirm or clear up any questions you might have by calling the rangers BEFORE you get to the park. In our experience, the rangers are very conscientious about checking your required gear and equipment. Be prepared to display all the required gear for the ranger's inspection.

Equipment, Gear, Etc.

All boats must be properly equipped for a long wilderness trip. Each boat must have the following equipment, and there can be NO EXCEPTIONS:

One U. S. Coast Guard Approved life vest per person, Type III or V. The vest must be in good shape.

One spare paddle for each canoe.

Bow and stern lines no less than 15 feet in length.

One bailer per boat. A sponge is also useful.

Adequate floatation. Some ABS boats have only minimal floatation. Check yours.

Potty. An RV-style flushable River Potty System is required. See below.

Your personal gear should include a set of boating clothes as well as a set of camp clothes. In addition, you should be prepared for the extremes of weather that can occur in this part of Texas. If your trip is in the spring or fall, the weather can be either like summer with temperatures in the high 90's or it can be like winter with cool days and frost at night. It can also rain at any time. In the "winter", from November to March, expect cold nights and cool days, and be alert to hypothermia.

A typical set of river clothes, that is, a "wet set" for wear while actually paddling the river, might consist of the following:

Long pants. Shorts offer no protection from the sun, rocks, or thorns, all of which you may encounter during the day. Pants should be of a fabric that dries quickly and provides comfort when wet. Wool, wool blends, and polypropylene clothes are good in summer or winter. Avoid jeans and other heavy cotton pants!

T-shirt. Cotton is okay; polypro is better -- cool in summer, warm in winter.

Long sleeve shirt. A lightweight shirt in summer will keep your arms from getting sunburned. In winter, a wool shirt will keep you warm, even if you are wet.

Tennis shoes, boat shoes, etc. Protect your feet and keep them warm while wet. Use wool or polypro socks. Fabric shoes do not become water-logged and have a chance to dry out. Have shoes that will not fall off while swimming!

Windbreaker, rain jacket, or rain suit. Even if it does not rain while you are paddling, a jacket to repel splash water will keep you comfortable.

Hat. Your head needs protection from the sun. The glare in this part of the state is blinding. Also, your head, neck, and face will sunburn quickly without some cover. A broad-brim hat is recommended. Have a chin strap or string to tie your hat on -- the winds will take your hat away, or you may lose it in a rapid.

Bandanna. On hot days, this is a blessing. Wear it around your neck to keep the sun off. Wet it and wipe your face in coolness.

Other gear that you will need for the trip includes these items:

Sunglasses. Have a strap to hold them on.

Canteen or water bottle. This should be accessible from your paddling position. A two liter plastic soda bottle makes a good one.

Small, water-tight box for personal items, camera, film, sun screen, maps, toilet paper, etc. This box should be small and accessible during the day.

Something to carry that day's lunch in. This avoids rummaging through your packed gear at a lunch stop. It should be water-proof. A small cooler works well.

Water jugs. This is very important! Each boat should carry from 5 to 8 gallons of water. These containers should be rugged and have a good closure. Two or more containers are recommended in order to better balance the weight in your boat.

Extra rope, duct tape, and a sponge.

For evenings, layover days, and other times that you are "in camp," another set of gear is recommended. This "dry set" for camp and hiking should include:

Long pants. Hiking in the desert means dealing with plants and shrubs that bite, stick, scratch, and claw at your skin. Be prepared.

Long sleeve shirt. Also protect your bare arms.

Short sleeve shirt. For times of relative warmth and comfort.

Camp shoes. Something dry and comfortable to wear around the camp.

Hiking shoes or boots. The terrain away from the river bank is full of rocks and cactus which will penetrate your lightweight shoes. A shoe with a hard sole and good support is essential for any climbing or hiking.

Swim suit and / or shorts. If you want to wade in the hot springs, you will need something suitable.

Coat, heavy jacket, or parka. The weather can be cold in the evenings and early morning.

Your camping gear should be similar to that for any other camping experience. The typical gear includes:

Tent. A small one is recommended -- you do have to get all of this gear in your canoe!

Ground cloth.

Sleeping bag or bed roll.

Pad or air mattress.

Small folding chair or camp stool. You will get very tired of sitting on the ground.

Small gas stove and fuel.

Cook kit and utensils.

Garbage bags. Carry all trash out!

Personal items. Soap, toothbrush, etc.

Flashlight and spare batteries.

A couple of luxury items, if you can manage to squeeze them in, are a table and a cot. The roll up type are a reasonable expense for the convenience and comfort that they provide.

Every trip of an expedition nature such as this should also include some special equipment that the trip leader is usually responsible for obtaining and ensuring that it is along. This gear is:

First Aid Kit. Be able to handle minor irritants such as headaches, colds, and sore throats, as well as big time emergencies such as sprains and broken limbs. Plant and animal stings are common in this country.

Safety Kit. Know your whitewater river rescue techniques, and bring the necessary rescue equipment.

Repair kit and tools. Bring an emergency set just in case.

Firepan. IF you plan to make a fire, take a firepan and pack out all unburned charcoal and wood.

Lantern. Emergency lighting may be needed in some night situations, otherwise, enjoy the night sky.

Machete. This emergency tool is useful in clearing brush and cane to give access to springs and portage trails.

One final comment about gear and equipment should mention things that definitely **do not** belong on a trip:

Pets. This is no place for them.

Radios. Enjoy the sounds and silence of the earth and its natural environment for these few days.

Controlled substances: Marijuana, cocaine, etc. are nothing but trouble. The abuse of alcohol is likewise out of place. Do not endanger the others on the trip who may have to rescue you when you have injured yourself because you were stoned. In addition, a bust on either side of the border will put innocent people through a lot of misery.

A bad disposition. Approach the stresses of a trip like this with a long sense of humor and tolerance of the weaknesses of your companions. They may be the one chance of rescue you have if you need it. Remember that you are here to have fun!

Containers and Packing

Your gear should be carried in sturdy, waterproof containers. Anything that can be damaged by moisture should be protected since there is always chance that it will get wet.

There are many kinds of containers that can be and are used on these kinds of trips. Some are inexpensive, but adequate. Others are expensive, durable, and adequate. Some of the more common types are "Bill's Bags," plastic paint buckets, plastic olive jars, and large ammo boxes. Invest in good containers or bags. Do not expect plastic trash bags to be sufficient. A night in a

Tables and chairs, though bulky and somewhat heavy, can make for a more pleasant camp on the river. Let's sit down for dinner!

wet sleeping bag is what you deserve if your gear is not properly protected.

When you have put all your gear together, pack everything and place it in your canoe. A trial run before you leave for the trip will tell if you are taking too much. It may also help you to pack your boat more efficiently.

You will be carrying a lot of equipment and weight on the trip, so it is important to distribute the weight in your boat evenly. Trim is important to the overall handling characteristics of your boat, and that extra bit of maneuverability may keep you off the rocks.

It is wise to remember that in the event that you capsize, you will want your gear bags and containers to stay in the boat. Tie ropes or use shock cords in an "X" fashion between the thwarts of the gear areas to secure your equipment.

Food

It is hard to elaborate here since each person has his own favorites. In general, plan your food supplies as if you were going on an eight day backpacking trip. Keep everything simple, light, and small. Freeze-dried and dehydrated foods are best, although an occasional canned luxury is permissible.

One dish dinners or stews are good, quick, and easy.

Lunches can be made of cheese, crackers, summer sausage, tuna, fruit, etc. Breakfast needs to be quick and easy, especially on paddling days. Instant oatmeal and fruit is good. Make your big meal in the evenings, and splurge on breakfast and lunch on the layover days.

Many easy-to-fix packaged foods are available in regular grocery stores. Things like Lipton's Pasta and Sauce make a good base for a camp casserole.

Refrigerated items can be taken if you know how to pack your cooler, however refrigeration and ice can be a mess and add unnecessary weight. Plan carefully.

No one is going to starve to death or not benefit from a simple diet. Keep your meal planning easy and tasty. You will have a hearty appetite after a day of paddling or hiking.

River Potty System

Nothing spoils the experience of a wilderness campsite faster than an over-used latrine area with remnant toilet tissue lying around. The unfortunate result of the increased traffic on the Rio Grande has been the fouling of several of the more popular camping areas. In order to remedy this situation, the National Park Service now requires all commercial outfitters and private river parties to carry out their solid human waste.

All river users are required to carry out solid human waste in a system compatible with RV dump stations, or by using a "blue-bag" system which chem-

This discreetly situated toilet is a certified RV-style river potty. Small enough to be carried in a canoe, yet rated at 50 uses.

ically alters the bag's contents into an inert substance. The previous systems which used bags and "rocket boxes" are no longer permitted on the river.

If you do not own an RV flushable system, bagless systems may be rented from local outfitters, including Desert Sports (432-371-2727) in Terlingua. The RV flush style systems can be emptied at Rio Grande Village, most RV parks and state parks.

The most popular "blue-bag" systems are the Restop or Wag Bag single-use bag systems.

The Restop uses a patented "bag within a bag" design to safely contain and neutralize human waste. The outer bag is a Mylar gas-impervious bag. Polymers and deodorizers used in the inside bag. The Restop system contains the odor as well as the waste, and it provides a user-friendly and pleasant means to pack out solid waste. Ample toilet paper and a moist antiseptic towlette are included with each single use system.

For your convenience, the Restop or Wag Bag single-use bag systems can be purchased at park bookstores in Big Bend National Park. They are also available from retail stores and online.

The Castolon Area

The valley of the Rio Grande in the western half of the Big Bend National Park has been an area of settlement and economic activity for over a century. The focal point of this activity was the community that is now known as Castolon. Castolon played a central role in the development of the floodplain of the Rio Grande from Terlingua Creek to the Johnson Ranch into a commercial farming region in support of the mining operations of the Terlingua district. With the closure of the Terlingua mines in the 1940's and the creation of the national park at the same time, Castolon has become the center of the tourist activity in this somewhat remote and less developed part of the Big Bend National Park. Even today, the Castolon Store still provides the best treat for visitors to the area -- ice cream.

The Castolon floodplain was relatively unpopulated until the late 19th century. The area is somewhat secluded because it lies in a pocket formed by the mountains along this section of the river. The Sierra Ponce is a formidable barrier along the south side of the Rio Grande. With its companion formation the Mesa de Anguila, the Sierra Ponce effectively separates the Castolon area from northern Chihuahua and the historic San Carlos area. Although Castolon lies between the eastern and western branches of the Comanche Trail, these natural barriers made it easier for the marauding Comanches, and Apaches before them, to go around the Castolon area, rather than through the area. Raiding parties descended on northern Mexico through the Paseo de Chisos to the east, while trading parties visited San Carlos via the ford at Lajitas to the west[18].

It was this proximity to the Comanche Trail, however, that first brought the Castolon area into the historical record, at least the historical record of the United States. After the Mexican War which established the Rio Grande as the boundary between the United States and Mexico, the United States assumed the responsibility for the pacification of the frontier along its borders. Since the raids into Mexico by the Comanches, Kiowas and Apaches, among others, originated in the United States, the United States was obligated by the treaty that ended the war to prevent hostile attacks on Mexico from within its territory. As a result, the U. S. Army sent a boundary survey party into the area, that is now known as Castolon, in 1852.

Lt. Duff C. Green and Marine Tyler Wickham Chandler led a small troop of soldiers east from Lajitas, circumventing the Mesa de Anguila and the imposing canyon that he called the Grand Canon San Carlos and descending Terlingua Creek, called Lates Lengua Creek at that time[125], to the Rio Grande floodplain. They camped for two days below the mouth of the canyon at a site that Green called Vado de Fleche, "the ford of arrows." One of the goals of the boundary survey was to scout the area for suitable locations for military encampments from which the army could patrol the border. Among the features that Green noted at this site was the broad valley that could be cultivated in support of a military post[120].

By 1860, it was imperative that the United States assert its influence in the Big Bend in order to curtail the hostile activities of the tribes of the Great Plains. In July, 1860, Colonel Robert E. Lee, the commander of the U. S. Army in Texas, sent 2Lt. William Echols into the area to find a site for a fort on the Rio Grande near the Comanche Trail. Echols confirmed the earlier assessment of Lt. Green, and he described the place in the floodplain near Alamo Creek as a good location for the military post. He noted, in particular, that the site had a fine valley for cultivation. In addition, Echols reported that the local Mexican residents of the area were strongly supportive of the plan for a fort since they could supply fresh produce for the fort just as the farmers of San Carlos and the Ojinaga-Presidio area were doing for Fort Davis[117]. Unfortunately, the Civil War intervened the next year and the military development along the Rio Grande was halted.

After the Civil War, the U. S. Army returned to Fort Davis in June, 1867 in order to safeguard the frontier of West Texas against Indian predations. In 1870, the Black Seminole Indian Scouts were enlisted at Fort Clark and fought the Comanches and Apaches from the Pecos to the Big Bend. In August, 1879, soldiers were stationed at Camp Pena Colorado near Marathon, and in March, 1885, Camp Neville Springs was established in the foothills of the Chisos Mountains. The presence of the army troops in the Big Bend brought an end to the attacks by the hostile bands. The transcontinental railroad was completed through the area in 1882, and settlers began to establish ranches in the region.

The Early Ranchers

Among the most prominent of the early ranchers in the Big Bend was John T. Gano. Gano had come to the Big Bend in 1879 while working for his father's company, R. M. Gano and Son[67]. Working in conjunction with the surveyors of Presidio County, Gano became familiar with the land in the Big Bend, and in 1885, John, his brother Clarence and E. L. Gage organized the Estado Land and Cattle Company of Dallas. They purchased 55,000 acres in survey Block G4 where they established the G4 Ranch. Headquartered at Oak Spring in the drainage below the Window of the Chisos Basin, the G4 Ranch extended from Terlingua Creek to the Chisos Mountains, and from Agua Fria Mountain on the north to the Rio Grande where a line camp was established at the mouth of Terlingua Creek[67].

Above average rains in the Big Bend during early 1880's produced fields of green grass in the desert and an abundance of water from the springs. These weather conditions, which filled the region with succulent vegetation, enticed the new ranchers to bring large herds to the region. In May, 1885, the Gano brothers drove a herd of 2,000 cattle from Dallas to the G4 Ranch, and by the end of the summer, that number had increased to 6,000 head. By 1891, the G4 Ranch had 30,000 head of cattle, making it one of the largest cattle ranches in West Texas[120].

The G4 Ranch managers did not understand the nature of the West Texas environment. While today, it is generally accepted that the range in West Texas can handle cattle on a ratio of 40 to 50 acres per head, the Gano brothers overstocked their ranch at two acres per head of cattle. The resources of the land were severely overburdened and the ranchers did not anticipate the changes in the rain patterns that were ahead. In a precipitation cycle that is familiar today, which produced ten droughts between 1892 to 1980, drought hit the Big Bend in 1885 and, again, in 1886. Dry conditions returned in the early 1890's and, weakened by drought and crippled by other problems, the G4 Ranch was forced to disband in 1895[67].

In addition to the Anglo Texans, Mexicans were also attracted to the area at this time by the grazing lands and the abundant spring water in the Big Bend. Ranchers from San Carlos, a military-agricultural colony fourteen miles south of the Rio Grande, grazed their cattle on the chino grass and other native grasses that were plentiful across the border in Texas. Eventually, many of them built homes and established ranches in the area. These ranchers, including Santiago Baisa, Roman de la O, Felix Gomez and Ramon Molinar in the Castolon area, settled in Texas and their arrival marked the beginnings of the first wave of Mexican immigration into the Big Bend[18].

In 1892, a decision of the District Court played a major role in the settlement of the Castolon area. On April 6, 1892, the State of Texas recovered Block 16 of the GH&SA Survey in a ruling that stated that the railroads had been assigned too much land as a result of allocations that were based on excessive and unnecessary mileage. The state then made the land available for sale as sectionalized school lands. The General Land Office surveyed the valley from Santa Elena Canyon to the site of the Johnson Ranch into thirty-six long, narrow sections, numbered one through thirty-six, instead of one mile square sections, so that potential landowners would have access to the river and the fertile floodplain. Initially, the Mexican American settlers in the lower Big Bend, who established themselves in the floodplain between Terlingua Creek and Castolon, did not attempt to acquire title to the land where they settled, but eventually, they did file on the land. All of theearlylandownersinBlock16wereMexicanAmericans[5]

The Hernandez Store

At the the turn of the 20th century, the most notable resident of what is now the Castolon area was Cipriano Hernandez. Although his surname is believed to have been Pacheco[21], Cipriano, who was born about 1845 in Camargo, Chihuahua, a city about 130 miles south of Ojinaga, lived with a family named Hernandez and he assumed their name as his own. Hernandez had married the fourteen year old Juanita Silvas of Camargo in 1890[21], and he immigrated to Shafter, Texas in the mid-1890's to work in the silver mines[5]. The need to provide for his family may have been the motivation for the 50 year old Hernandez to find work in the mining operations, and their son Guadalupe Silvas Hernandez was born in Shafter in 1896[54].

After the mines opened in the Terlingua area, Cipriano Hernandez recognized that the Terlingua mining district would need the same kind of supporting enterprises that he had seen in Presidio for the mines at Shafter. The workers at the mines would need fresh meat and fresh vegetables, and the floodplain east of Terlingua Creek could be farmed to provide those goods. In 1901, Hernandez leased sections 17 and 18 of Block 16 for two years[5]. These sections, which are east of Castolon and near what is now called Smuggler's Canyon and the Buenos Aires Campsite, were less suitable for farming, but more appropriate for raising goats. Hernandez built his home at the base of the gravel hill in section 14 and farmed the adjacent floodplain of sections 13 and 14. Eventually, in 1910, Hernandez filed for title on sections 13 and 14[5].

By 1903, Hernandez had completed the construction of his home. As the first permanent structure in area, the adobe wall house was built on a foundation of river cobblestones. The roof was made of cottonwood vegas and a river cane ceiling[140]. The sturdiness of the construction is such that the house, now known as the Alvino House, is over one hundred years old and is the oldest adobe structure still standing in Big Bend National Park[20].

Hernandez called his community Santa Helena[1], most likely because of the magnificent canyon that is such a prominent landmark visible throughout the valley. On this fertile floodplain, Hernandez and his small community grew beans, squash, pumpkins and watermelons which he sold to the local community and to the miners of Terlingua from a small store which he set up in the east end of his home[83]. He expanded his store to include other essential items that were needed by the local community, such as spices, sugar, flour, corn meal and salt[5]. Hernandez also irrigated the floodplain in order to grow wheat, corn, oats and cereal grains for mule feed for the haulers who worked for the mines[1]. The store prospered as Hernandez served customers from both sides of the Rio Grande.

Others joined Hernandez in this second phase of the first wave of Mexican immigration into the Big Bend. In response to the mining boom in the region, a fairly large number of farmers saw the opportunity to use local agriculture to feed the mining towns[18]. About 1903, Agapito Carrasco settled a group of six Mexican families a mile downstream from Hernandez at a com-

The Alvino House was originally built by Cipriano Hernandez and later lived in by the Sublett family before becoming the home of Alvino Ybarra. Santa Elena Canyon is seen in the distance.

munity which he called El Ojito[68]. El Ojito was located in section 15 of Block 16, and Carrasco filed on the land in 1915[5]. In 1908, Ruperto Chavarria, the Texas-born son of a Mexican immigrant ranch laborer, brought a larger group of immigrants to the west bank of Alamo Creek to form the community of La Coyota[1]. About 1910, Patricio Marquez filed on section 12, the tract adjacent to Hernandez' farm[5]. In all, about 200 to 300 residents, some of whom wanted to take advantage of the economic activities of mining in the area, but many of whom had left the social upheavals caused by the Mexican Revolution, came to the lower Big Bend and inhabited a string of subsistence farming communities along the river which included Santa Helena, El Ojito, La Coyota, Terlingua Abaja, and Buenos Aires[68].

The interest in the land of Block 16 along the Rio Grande was largely limited to Mexicans and Mexican Americans. Prior to 1915, only Mexicans had filed to homestead the sections of Block 16[5]. However, the success of the floodplain farming in the Santa Helena area was noticed by rancher Clyde Buttrill. Clyde and his brother Lou operated ranches in the Rosillos Mountains[1], north of the Chisos Mountains, and Buttrill believed that he could produce alfalfa and other winter grains for his cattle ranch on the floodplain[1]. With this plan in mind, in 1914, he purchased section 12 from Patricio Marquez and sections 13 and 14 from Cipriano Hernandez[5].

Upon the sale of his home, store and farmland, Cipriano Hernandez, who was 69 years old in 1914, moved to Terlingua Abaja[1]. He and his son Guadalupe, who was 18 years old, opened a large mercantile business there because he felt that it was advantageous to be closer to the mining operations in Terlingua[68]. It also allowed the aging father to give a helping hand to his son who had only the year before married Teresa Baeza[21]. The proceeds from the sale were sufficient to permit the investment in the mercantile store at Terlingua Abaja, but Hernandez soon found significant competition in the area. Within five years, two other stores

opened in the area, and it appears that Hernandez was unable to succeed with his new venture. By 1920, both Cipriano and his son Guadalupe lived next door to each other in Terlingua Abaja and worked as general laborers[150]. In 1930, Cipriano Hernandez, now 85 years old, was retired and lived in Terlingua Abaja with his wife Juana, 54, and his mother-in-law, Juliana Silvas, an 80 year old widow[50]. Cipriano and his mother-in-law died while living at Terlingua Abaja, but the other family members had to abandon their property in Terlingua Abaja about 1944 when the land was acquired for the Big Bend National Park. Guadalupe Hernandez and his family were living on the east side of Terlingua Creek in 1930 near the Sublett farm where he worked as a farm manager[54]. After the creation of the national park, the Hernandez families settled in Odessa, Texas[21].

The Buttrill Farm

Clyde Buttrill came to the Big Bend in 1884 when his father William Buttrill moved his wife Ann and two sons, Lucius and Clyde, to Brewster County from Bee County in the Coastal Bend of Texas. After their father's death in the early 1890's, the Buttrill brothers ranched in the Rosillos Range with their cousin Jim P. Wilson. In 1908, Clyde Buttrill bought a ranch of his own in the Nine Points Mountain area which he ranched until he acquired the Rio Grande floodplain land in 1914[140]. In the spring of 1914, Clyde Buttrill, then 34 years old, hired the 44 year old James L. Sublett of Sweetwater[83], a well-respected farmer who was experienced in irrigation techniques and had experience with railroad machinery and landscaping, to manage the farm along the river.

James L. Sublett was born in Alabama in July, 1869 and had moved to Texas by the early 1890's[54]. He married his Texas-born wife Malissa, "Belle," in 1893 and their first child Wallace was born in September, 1894. In 1900, Sublett and his family were living in Sweetwater, Texas where he worked as a day laborer. Sublett's experiences were quite varied since, in 1910, he worked as a butcher in a retail shop in Sweetwater[54]. Along the way, he also gained the experience in farming and machinery operations that convinced Buttrill to employ him[154].

Buttrill wanted Sublett to clear the floodplain and to grow alfalfa and other feed crops there[1]. In order to achieve the levels of production that Buttrill expected, Sublett introduced mechanized farming techniques to the area, including the first irrigation system in the area and a wheat threshing machine[68]. Sublett and his family moved into the former Hernandez house and he hired local Mexican laborers, including Leandro Silvas and Benjamin Sanchez, to plant the crops of wheat, corn, alfalfa and other feed crops[1]. The local laborers eventually planted a large assortment of crops that included wheat, corn, alfalfa, Irish potatoes, sweet potatoes and peanuts[154].

Sublett was also asked to operate the store which was in a room of the house, and, according to his agreement with Buttrill, Sublett could keep the profits from the store operation[5]. Realizing that the store operation needed more space than the room in the house could provide, Sublett soon moved the store from the house to a larger building on the site now known as "Old Castolon" which is across the road from the modern Cottonwood Campground[83]. The operations of the farm and the store were so successful that by February, 1916, Sublett and Buttrill had become partners in the enterprise[68].

The political and social instability in northern Mexico, caused by the Mexican Revolution, began to affect the border lands by 1916. On October 15, 1916, the United States War Department leased about four acres of land near Santa Helena (modern Castolon) from Clyde Buttrill and established Camp Santa Helena with a cavalry troop for the protection of the local residents of the mining district. Elements of the 5th, 6th and 8th Cavalry took up residence at this remote outpost on the site originally selected for a military fort in 1852[1].

Ultimately, Buttrill had no desire to contend with the tensions along the border[1]. In 1918, Clyde Buttrill sold his sections in Block 16 to a trio of Texas Rangers who had been assigned to Santa Helena area to help curtail the border raids resulting from Mexican Revolution. Texas Rangers Carroll Bates, Will C. Jones and M. T. Junker acquired sections 10, 11, 12, 13 and 14, Block 16 GH&SA Railway Survey[5]. Buttrill returned to ranching in the Rosillos Mountains. He had served as the Treasurer of Brewster County in 1914 and 1915, he was active in the the community at Marathon although he never married, and he died in May, 1932 of pneumonia at age 53[140].

After Buttrill sold his interests in the farming operation at Santa Helena and dissolved his partnership with James Sublett, Sublett established a new farm about two miles upstream in a partnership with Albert W. Dorgan[68]. At the same time, border patrol activities kept the Texas Rangers busy and unable to manage the farming operations. In addition, friction between the cavalry troops stationed at Camp Santa Helena and the

The Sublett store was moved to the "Old Castolon" site about 1916, and it was the site of La Harmonia store until 1921.

Texas Rangers under Carroll Bates created problems on the Texas side of the border. The dispute seems to have been related to the disposal of manure, garbage and refuse from the cavalry camp on the Bates property[5], but in any case, the problems were sufficient enough that Bates and his partners decided to sell their land. In 1919, the partnership of Howard E. Perry and Wayne R. Cartledge acquired sections 12, 13 and 14 of Block 16[5]. Over the course of the next fifty years, Wayne Cartledge would become the most prominent person in the area that we now know as Castolon.

Sublett - Dorgan Farm

Although Clyde Buttrill chose to abandon the farming of the floodplain after only a few years, James L. Sublett continued to believe in the potential of the area. After the sale of the Buttrill farm to Perry and Cartledge, Sublett re-established his farm a few miles upstream from Castolon on land he bought from Tom and Charlie Metcalf[68]. In the fall of 1918, the 48 year old Sublett formed a partnership with Albert W. Dorgan, a man 18 years his junior[153], and acquired four sections of land west of Alamo Creek. They called their business the Grand Canyon Company in deference to the former name of Santa Elena Canyon which dominates the southwestern horizon[180].

The Metcalf brothers had owned land which was known locally as Rancho Steele since previously it had been occupied by Leonidas V. Steele. Steele had acquired the property through his marriage to the daughter of Miguel de la O, a prominent local rancher[1]. L. V. Steele, who had been born in Indiana in July, 1840, was known as a mining prospector, however, by 1900, the 60 year old Steele was working as a freighter[151]. Apparently, he was fairly successful in his business ventures since he had six servants working at his ranch. However, Steele had recently lost his wife of 32 years, and, perhaps because of this, he chose to end his association with the lower Big Bend. About 1902, Steele married Anna Walters, a single parent with a young daughter, and moved to Tom Green County. In 1910, Steele and his 44 year old wife Anna lived in the Water Valley Settlement near San Angelo with their son Fred, who was born in 1905, and his seventeen year old stepdaughter Jessie Walters. L. V. Steele died some time prior to 1920, and Annie and son Fred continued to live and work in San Angelo[151].

With the departure of L. V. Steele from the area, the land around Rancho Steele became available for homesteading. M. C. Cantu Terrazas filed to homestead Section 4, the tract where the Steele house was located, in 1906, but Cantu Terrazas never completed his application for title[5]. In 1910, Miguel de la O filed on the adjacent tract, Section 5[5]. Subsequently, Charles E. Metcalf filed on Section 4 in 1915, and he probably filed on the remaining nearby sections as well since by 1918, he had acquired the title to four sections. In the fall of 1918, Metcalf sold Sections 4, 5, 6 and 7 in Block 16 to the partnership of James Sublett and Albert Dorgan[2].

Charles Metcalf was one of six brothers of the Metcalf family who came to West Texas from California in the 1890's. His father Louis Metcalf moved his wife Josephine and young son James to Lake County, California, north of San Francisco, between 1855 and 1860 from Arkansas where he worked as a farmer. The family grew to include three daughters and eight sons by 1880. However, by the 1890's the family had moved to the Ozona area in Crockett County, Texas where, in 1900, their widowed mother lived with her daughter Maggie next to her son George and his family. Yet, even at age 64, Josephine Metcalf listed her occupation as a stock raiser. The other Metcalf brothers, including Charles, Robert, Fred and Wilsey, the youngest at age 20, worked as stock men and lived together at a home in Ozona with the older brother Tom[152].

By 1910, the Metcalf family was well established in West Texas, though not especially prosperous. Tom Metcalf, age 44, was working as a ranch stockman in Val Verde County. Robert, age 35, lived in Ozona near his brother Charles where he worked as an odd job laborer. Charles Metcalf had married in 1905 and in 1910, at age 40, he was employed as a tinner in a tin shop in Ozona where he lived with his twenty-five year old wife Bettie Lea and their young sons Wade, age 4, and Fred, age 2. Their mother Josephine Metcalf, 74, lived with son George and his family at this time. George Metcalf, 38, was employed as an odd job laborer in Ozona to support his wife of 15 years J. Beulah, 31, their daughter Lessie, 11, and their son Condra, 13[152].

About 1915, Charles Metcalf became interested in the lower Big Bend. He filed on the land along the Rio Grande where L. V. Steele had lived and, with his brother Tom, established a homestead on four sections west of Alamo Creek[5]. Whether their intention was to stay in the area and build a ranch or to simply remain long enough on the land to gain title is not known. However, when the opportunity to sell out came shortly after their three years residency requirement was met, the Metcalf brothers took Sublett's offer, and in 1918, they sold him their land and left the area. They certainly were not the first or only individuals to use the homestead laws to speculate on real estate in the Big Bend.

In 1920, Charles Metcalf and his family lived in Alpine. He was the manager of a steam laundry and his son Fred was a telegraph office messenger boy. His wife Betty kept the household of Wade, Fred, daughters Norine, Elizabeth and young son Charley. By 1930, Charles Metrcalf had moved the family to a farm in Hill County, near Whitney along the Brazos River and north of Waco where he could live out his retirement years along side the farm of his recently married son Fred[152].

The years that James Sublett spent working with Clyde Buttrill convinced him that the Rio Grande floodplain held extraordinary opportunities. It may

This Big Bend National Park base map[7] shows the sections of Block 16 around Castolon.

even have been Sublett who persuaded the Metcalf brothers to abandon the floodplain. Immediately upon acquiring the sections from Charles Metcalf, Sublett went to work to establish both a farming operation on the floodplain and a mercantile store just as he had done on the Buttrill land. Sublett converted a two room adobe house, the former home of Tom Metcalf and previously the headquarters of Rancho Steele, into a small store. The Subletts lived in this small house at the foot of the hill until he could build a larger home on top of the nearby hill[1].

Eventually, Sublett brought in his son-in-law Fred Spann to manage the store[1]. The Sublett store served the local residents along both sides of the Rio Grande and it even provided goods and supplies to the Mexican soldiers encamped across the Rio Grande when items were difficult to obtain through their normal channels[1]. Competition from the store established by Wayne Cartledge at Castolon, however, was strong, and in 1927, the store operated by Sublett and Spann at Rancho Steele was closed[1].

But, in 1918, the construction of the facilities that Sublett would need for the farm was underway. Sublett hired Alvino Ybarra and Cisto Avila, two local stone masons, to build him a home on top of the hill and a smaller house for his farmhands below it[1]. This three room rock and adobe house was built across the intervening valley to the southwest from the Metcalf house.

Albert Dorgan and his wife lived there until he built a home a decade later on the mesa to the north[2]. The Sublett Stone Farm house, as it is known, is located on a low terrace about 100 feet north of the paved Park road. It has two rooms of equal size of about 250 square feet each, separated by a "dog trot" breezeway[29]. The walls of the breezeway are adobe on the lower half and stone above. The construction is rubble stone masonry with mud mortar, and the masonry is angular blocks of local stone. The simple door and window openings are made with dimensional lumber sills. Today, all of the headers and jambs of the Sublett Farm House are missing, but the walls still stand about eight feet tall[29].

Sublett built his adobe home on top of the small hill above the store. Although the Sublett house was still intact in 1949 when the International Boundary and Water Commission survey crews worked in the area[30], today, it is a severely deteriorated adobe ruin.

The Dorgan House

Sublett's partner in the floodplain farming venture was a 30 year old Albert W. Dorgan. In 1918, there was a burst of construction as the partnership tried to get the farm established and in operation. Initially, Dorgan and his wife lived in the three room rock and adobe house built across the arroyo to the southwest from the other buildings of the Sublett Complex. Subsequently, during the next ten years or so, Dorgan supervised the construction of an elaborate house on the mesa about a half mile northeast of Sublett's home. This magnificent structure would become one of the most significant architectural structures in the Big Bend.

As for Albert Dorgan himself, little is actually known. Some sources say that he was a German immigrant who had worked in Detroit, Michigan as an architect and a city planner[1]. What we do know from the census records is that Dorgan was living in Lansing, Michigan in 1910 and he was working as a clerk in the "state building" office. Far from being a German immigrant, though, his father was born in Canada and his mother was born in Michigan. Dorgan himself was born in Michigan, as well[153]. Almost all of the Dorgan families in Michigan at that time were of Irish descent.

Although Dorgan was a prominent resident in the lower Big Bend for over thirty years, his background is quite mysterious and vague. Oddly, even though his partner and neighbor, James Sublett, is well represented in the census records, Dorgan is no where to be found in the records after 1910. Yet, we do know that he was active in the Big Bend as late as 1943. In the fall of 1934, Albert Dorgan wrote to Secretary of the Interior Harold Ickes offering his resume and his services to the NPS if they would establish an international park in the Big Bend. He described himself as a former aviator in World War I[164]. The records of the Big Bend National Park also indicate that Dorgan wrote a letter in 1940 to Cordell Hull, the United States Secretary of State, proposing the creation of a Pan American Peace Park in the Big Bend area of Texas. He was also on contract with the International Boundary and Water Commission as late as 1943 to measure rainfall and operate a stream gauging station on the Rio Grande prior to the creation of the park[39].

Though certainly not a recluse in his long residence in the Big Bend, Albert Dorgan revealed little of his own background for the record. He was not the first, nor the last, person to retreat to the remote regions of the Big Bend to seek the unquestioned anonymity that the desert can provide. Yet, perhaps the most revealing thing about the elusive Dorgan is the magnificent home that he built on the high terrace above the Rio Grande floodplain.

In a departure from the typical buildings of the region which consisted of one or more small rectangu-

Photo Credit: Louis F. Aulbach

The ruins of the Dorgan house which sits on the gravel terrace above the flood plain.

lar rooms of ten to twelve feet in width, the Dorgan house had a relatively huge main room measuring thirty feet square. Three smaller, and more typical, rooms and a porch were built around this central living area to make a total floor space of about 1,200 square feet[29]. The key factor in determining the width of the traditional house structure was the scarcity of long wooden beams for the roof. Vegas, or tree trunks, longer than twelve feet were rare in the lower Big Bend and it was expensive to bring special lumber to the area. Dorgan's design solved this problem with his ingenious use of a central fireplace in the main room.

A two-way fireplace in the center of the main room was a structural pier supporting four huge cottonwood log beams that extended to the corners of the house and formed a hipped, almost flat, roof with a large chimney at the apex. The fireplace supported the center of the roof and reinforced adobe corners of the room supported the other end of the ceiling beams. Smaller poles were then positioned from the walls to the main beams to create the roof[29].

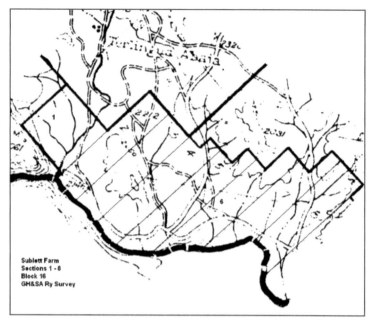

Sublett Farm
Sections 1 - 8
Block 16
GH&SA Ry Survey

The sections of Block 16 where the Sublett Farm was located[7].

The fireplace faced both the front entrance and the back of the large living room. It was unusually well-designed and made of very attractive native stone. Sections of petrified wood logs were placed vertically along their long axes and laid in cement mortar[29]. The flue appears to be constructed from fifty-five gallon steel barrels. Petrified trees can be found in a number of locations in the Big Bend, including near Bone Springs, in a canyon near the Grapevine Hills[107] and in Tornillo Flats[174], but the exact source of the stones for the chimney is not known.

Other features of the Dorgan house also show Dorgan's exceptional sense of design. The door jambs and the lintels over the windows and the main entrance were carefully selected, cured and hand-hewn logs with mortised, saw-cut joints that form segmental arches. The one-story adobe construction was set upon foundations and a floor of concrete. The walls of the house were plastered inside and out with a lime-based stucco[29]. The southeast side of the house opened to a covered terrace or ramada overlooking the floodplain with a picturesque view of the Chisos Mountains, Cerro Castellan and the Rio Grande valley.

In 1949, the Dorgan house was occupied by the survey crew for the International Boundary and Water Commission who were evaluating the Rio Grande watershed for possible dams[30]. Since that time, however, the Dorgan house has been unoccupied and largely left to deteriorate. Although the Rancho Estelle complex, which includes the Sublett Farm, the Stone Residence

and the Dorgan Residence, was added to the National Register of Historic Places in 1974[46], little was done to preserve the structural integrity of the Dorgan house until about 2003 when the eroding adobe walls were stabilized with a topping of plaster to prevent further "melting" of the walls.

La Coyota Community

When James Sublett devised his plans for a partnership with Albert Dorgan in order to clear the land near Rancho Steele and to establish a sophisticated, irrigated farm on the floodplain, he knew that there was also a readily available supply of farm labor in the area. From his four years of experience with the Buttrill farm, he knew that the La Coyota community could provide the workers he would need to operate the farm.

As early as 1900, the 57 year old Sipriano Chavarria and his family were living along the Rio Grande near Leonidas V. Steele at Rancho Steele[151]. In 1908, Sipriano's 31 year old son Ruperto Chavarria filed on section 9, Block 16 GH&SA Railway Survey[5] where he had established a community of about nine families in a village that they called La Coyota[68]. La Coyota was situated on the west bank of Alamo Creek and many of its immigrant residents were members of Chavarria's extended family[2]. Besides Ruperto Chavarria and his family, the other residents included the families of Atelano Pando, Tiburcio Garcia, Tiburcio Ramirez, Tomas Dominguez, Juan Silvas, Sabino Estorga, Patricio Dominguez and Mario Ramirez[1]. La Coyota was a settlement of a dozen or more houses in which "the Garcia family occupied the large houses on the mesa while members of the Chavarria family occupied the houses scattered at the foot of the hills along Alamo Creek[5]."

Although, as the manager of the Buttrill farm, Sublett mainly raised feed crops such as wheat, corn and alfalfa for Buttrill's Ranch operations, he was convinced by Albert Dorgan to develop a truck farm to provide fresh vegetables to the mining district around Terlingua[1]. This type of farm was labor intensive then, as it is today, but the farm was successful, and for many years, it provided employment for a large number of Mexican families at La Coyota and the other communities along the river. In addition to employment on the Sublett farm, the families at La Coyota farmed small plots along Alamo Creek for themselves or they cut and hauled wood for the Chisos mines[2].

Ruperto Chavarria himself prospered during his career with the Sublett operations. With his wife Angelita, he raised a family in La Coyota, and he advanced from his position as a general farm laborer in 1920 to become a farm manager by 1930[50]. Having acquired the title to the land he had homesteaded, Ruperto Chavarria sold the land around La Coyota to the state of Texas in 1942[5], when he was 65 years old, for the creation of Big Bend National Park.

A survey in 1964 found the La Coyota community in ruins[8]. Ten adobe and stone ruins lay clustered on the east bank of Alamo Creek where it empties into the Rio Grande floodplain, and the ruins of several homes were located along the west bank of Alamo Creek. The ruins of an old church were still visible, in 1980, in the middle of an old field a mile upstream on the east bank[2]. At the turn of the 21st century, the La Coyota cemetery, on a lonely point of the upland mesa, is still visited by the relatives of those residents buried in the twenty-two deteriorating graves[17].

La Harmonia Company

La Harmonia Company and the seemingly peculiar partnership between the aging industrialist Howard Perry and the young accountant Wayne Cartledge is largely a product of the fertile, if not somewhat ruthless, business mind of Perry. Perry was a successful boot manufacturer in Chicago when, about 1900, he received title to a parcel of land in Brewster County in payment for a debt[1]. This land happened to include the cinnabar outcrop discovered by two local cowboys, T. Devine McKinney and J. M. Parker, who had tried unsuccessfully to mine the ore. Perry sued McKinney and Parker and won the right to exploit the cinnabar claim on his own[1]. With the assistance of Austin attorney Eugene Cartledge, Perry secured a $50,000 loan to capitalize the Chisos Mining Company, and the two men incorporated the company on May 8, 1903[1]. The Chisos Mine went on to become the largest producer of mercury in the Terlingua Mining District, and Perry used every technique at his disposal to maximize the profits from his venture. The commercial farming and general merchandising business of La Harmonia in support of the mining operations were aspects of that plan.

Howard E. Perry was born in November, 1860 in Ohio to parents who were native to that state as well. By 1880, the 20 year old Perry had moved to the large commercial center of the Midwest, Chicago, and was renting a room while working in the city as a clerk. During the next twenty years, Perry found success and wealth in the wholesale boot business, and in 1900, at age 40, he and his wife of three years, Grace, lived in a stylish home on Prairie Avenue with two household servants. During the next decade, however, Perry turned his interest to the mining operations in Texas, and although he maintained his home in Chicago, by 1910, he was spending much of his time in Terlingua and he considered himself to be in the mining business[155].

Perry's attorney and partner in the Chisos Mining Company, Eugene Cartledge, was born in February, 1858 in Mississippi. By 1880, he was living with his uncle Roscoe Holmes in Bell County and attending college. By the turn of the century, the forty-two year old Cartledge had become a successful lawyer who lived in Austin with wife of seventeen years, Nancy, and their two sons and six daughters[156]. Cartledge used his influence with Perry to get a job for his oldest son Wayne, and by 1909, the twenty-two year old Wayne Rollins Cartledge had moved to Terlingua and had become an accountant and manager of the Chisos Mining Company[1].

Wayne Cartledge did well in his work with the Chisos Mine. He was appointed the postmaster of Terlingua on March 13, 1914[40]. And, over the decade or so that he worked for the mining company, Wayne Cartledge and Howard Perry developed a good business relationship[1]. In late 1918, the fifty-eight year old industrialist and the thirty-one year old mine manager formed a partnership which, eventually, they called La Harmonia Company[83]. It would be an enduring partnership that lasted until Perry's death in 1944[1].

As Perry and Cartledge envisioned it, the partnership involved the leasing of grazing lands, the purchase of farm land and the operation of a mercantile business. In the spring of 1919, Perry and Cartledge purchased the former Buttrill property from Carroll Bates and took over the operation of the store. Cartledge believed that to be successful they needed to diffuse the tensions that existed among the local residents and to promote peace and order[5]. With this goal in mind, they selected the "La Harmonia" name for their enterprise to give it an international flavor and to promote harmony among the contentious groups in the area, the cavalry troops, the Texas Rangers and the Mexican Americans[5].

Cartledge and Perry took over the former Sublett store with the idea of establishing a new and larger trading post. Under the new management, the store took on the characteristics of a frontier general store. They were able to offer a well balanced stock of merchandise through connections with the suppliers of the Chisos Mining Company, and, as a result, they attracted a large number of customers from the northern Mexican states of Coahuila and Chihuahua because it was so difficult to serve these remote locations from the interior of Mexico. In addition, La Harmonia served many smaller customers along the Rio Grande, and it was a wholesaler for many of the small Mexican stores in the region. Cartledge also became a middleman for the local candelilla wax processors and fur traders[5].

The La Harmonia Company store was located on the floodplain near the modern Cottonwood Campground. The store building has been restored in recent years, and it can be seen in the exhibit called "Old Castolon" that is across the paved road from the campground[83]. James Sublett had moved the store from his house, which is now known as the Alvino House, to this location about 1916 and operated the store there until Clyde Buttrill sold out.

The U. S. Army established a temporary camp in the Santa Helena area in late 1916, and the construction of a permanent camp was begun in 1919. In September, 1919, the army began the improvements to Camp Santa Helena which would eventually provide nine new structures, including two officer's quarters, a non-commissioned officer's quarters, a barracks with a mess hall, a lavatory, a recreation hall, a canteen, a grain shed, a stable and a water tower with a storage tank[1]. However, by the time the permanent camp was completed in 1920, the troops were reassigned and the new facilities were never used by the troops[68].

In 1921, the Army allowed Cartledge to use the new facilities at Camp Santa Helena[73]. He moved his store into the abandoned barracks from its location on the floodplain, and he and his employees took up residence in the officer's quarters and other buildings on the site[68]. In January, 1925, the War Department offered the military installation for sale, and Cartledge and Perry bought the nine buildings for $1,280 in April, 1926[68]. With the purchase of the abandoned camp, La Harmonia's headquarters were formally established on the site. Most of the buildings of Camp Santa Helena, and later La Harmonia Company, are still in use today and are operated as a park concession. Even, the comfort station and restrooms at modern Castolon were built as the latrine and shower facility for the troops of the U. S. Cavalry[113].

After La Harmonia Company was firmly settled in its new buildings and the farm was fully operational, the community of Santa Helena petitioned the government for a post office. On March 29, 1926, Richard W. Derrick, a farm manager for the company, was appointed postmaster[40]. However, since there already was a Santa Helena post office in Texas, the community changed its name to Castolon[68]. The village was named after the nearby Cerro Castellan, or Castolon Peak[68], a mountain displaying layers of vivid red volcanic rock. Castolon is thought to be a corruption of the Spanish word *castellan* which means the keeper or caretaker of

a castle. Other sources suggest that the area received its name from an early settler named Castulo who lived at a nearby spring[2]. From this time on, the area became Castolon, and it is called that today.

The other component of La Harmonia Company, in addition to the mercantile store, was the large scale farming of the floodplain. James Sublett had shown that the floodplain was extremely fertile and that commercial agriculture could be a profitable enterprise. Perry and Cartledge obviously had seen the potential for agricultural production, and with the acquisition of the former Buttrill sections, La Harmonia could take advantage of fields that had already been cleared of the thick riparian vegetation that becomes densely overgrown after only a few years of neglect. Today, the fields have been untended for over sixty years, and one can see the opportunity that attracted Perry and Cartledge.

La Harmonia Cotton Farming

Cipriano Hernandez showed that the floodplain could be commercially productive with his crops of fruits and vegetables. Buttrill and Sublett introduced large scale agriculture to the floodplain and raised feed crops in support of cattle operations. La Harmonia planned to use the farm to produce a cash crop. Initially, Cartledge planted wheat, just as Sublett had done, but since the price for wheat was in a decade long decline, Cartledge decided to grow cotton[1].

Cartledge wanted to create a fully integrated cotton operation in Castolon so, in addition to planting cotton, he also built a cotton gin on the site. Construction on the cotton gin and pumphouse building began in 1922[8]. Located at the entrance to what is now the Cottonwood Campground and across the road from the old Sublett store, the two story building was made of adobe blocks and it measured about sixty feet by fifty-five feet. A roof of corrugated steel covered the building whose floor was partly made of wood and partly earthen[8]. In the spring of 1923, Cartledge bought a cotton gin that was powered by a 1915 model steam engine and boiler which also drove the irrigation pumps for the fields[113].

The cotton gin was put in operation in October, 1923[1], but the output for that season was only three bales of cotton because Cartledge did not know how to operate the gin[1]. For the next season, Cartledge hired Richard W. Derrick to operate the cotton gin. Derrick was a store clerk in Terlingua[156] who had worked as a shipbuilder in Boston during World War I and was skilled in operating machinery. Within a short time, he had the cotton gin running. Once Derrick had the gin working smoothly, he hired Alvino Ybarra and trained him to run the cotton gin. With the gin operating around the clock, La Harmonia could produce 150 to 200 bales of cotton per season[1].

Cotton farming is a labor intensive enterprise and La Harmonia depended on the reliable source of farm workers from the border area. Many local families spent many years in the employ of La Harmonia, and the company provided a stable source of income to them for over twenty years. The families living near Castolon who worked in cotton farming included the families of Alvino and Jorge Ybarra, Lazaro Hinojos, Amado Leyba, Francisco and Juan Silvas, Baldomiano and Guadalupe Avila, Florentino Garcia, Nacasio Chacon and Juan Medina[1].

Few of the Mexican American workers for La Harmonia Company, or any of the Anglo-owned businesses in the lower Big Bend at this time, received the recognition for their contribution to the success of the enterprise. One exception was Alvino Ybarra who operated the cotton gin and later became a trusted farm manager for the company[158].

Ybarra immigrated to the Big Bend in 1914 from Ocampo, Coahuila[1]. Like many of the one million refugees from the Mexican revolutions that began about 1910, the 24 year old Ybarra fled the upheavals of northern Mexico and came to Texas to find work and the chance to live in peace. When he arrived in the Big Bend, he went to work for James Sublett. Then, when Sublett moved to Rancho Steele in 1918, Ybarra moved into Sublett's house, the house built by Cipriano Hernandez, and expanded the house to accommodate his family and the families of his relatives Guadalupe Avila and George Valenzuela[1]. Ybarra lived at what has become known as the "Alvino House" from 1918 to 1957[73], and he worked for La Harmonia Company until it ceased operations and the land was turned over to the park.

After Richard Derrick trained Ybarra to operate the cotton gin in 1923, cotton production remained strong for a few years, however, in 1927, the farm was beset with losses due to a severe drought in the Big Bend and the erratic cotton prices on the world market[1]. The next year, 1928, La Harmonia found it hard to hire laborers to harvest crops when the government began a strict enforcement of immigration laws in the Big Bend[68]. The price of cotton continued to drop in 1928, and the cotton gin was permanently abandoned in 1929. The pumphouse was still used for irrigation, but, after 1929, cotton was harvested and sent to Fort Stockton for processing[8]. In 1942, La Harmonia ceased all cotton farming operations[1].

Between 1923 and 1942, La Harmonia produced 2,000 bales of cotton[68]. Yet, even in the best years of production, the farming operation was never profitable. During its twenty years of operation, it was the most productive farm in the entire region, however, La Harmonia never made more than $1,200 in any one year[1]. The Big Bend National Park acquired the cotton gin in 1961[8], and a survey of the park in 1964 found that the gin's rusting machinery was still in the old building. During the record flood in 1974, the remains of the cotton gin and its heavy machinery were washed into the Rio Grande and disappeared downstream[2].

Castolon is situated on a mesa-like bluff of gravels that were deposited during the Miocene Period about 10 million years before the present. The low plain of gravel is cut by many dry arroyos and this topography gives the area an appearance of rolling hills[5]. The buildings that make up Castolon are set prominently at the edge of the bluff and overlook the floodplain of the Rio Grande. With the La Harmonia Company structures as the center, a community of La Harmonia managers and employees grew up along the floodplain at base of the bluffs. By the late 1930's, the population of Castolon was 25 persons[68].

Wayne Cartledge, his wife Jennie and their son Eugene lived in the main house on the hill[5]. About a dozen Mexican American families who worked for La Harmonia Company lived in three or four clusters of adobe houses at the base of the hill[5]. The extended Ybarra family lived in the house at the base of the hill immediately to the southwest of the store. Juan, Liando and Chico Silva and their families lived about a half mile upstream from Castolon in a cluster of houses in the upper portion of section 13 which at one time had

The foundation of La Harmonia Company cotton gin can still be seen near the entrance to Cottonwood Campground.

Photo Credit: Louis F. Aulbach

Clyde O. Stephens shares a story with Linda Gorski. Stephens managed the Castolon Store for nearly a decade until 2002. He was an avid local historian of the Castolon area and was especially generous in sharing his knowledge of the region with visitors to the store.

Photo Credit: Louis F. Aulbach

been the Sublett residence[5]. Store manager Richard W. Derrick and his wife lived in an adobe home that he built on the alluvial flats below and east of the store in Castolon[8].

Richard Derrick was born in May, 1888, one of seven surviving children born to San Jacinto County, Texas farmer George Derrick and his wife Sarah[157]. By 1910, Derrick had left the farm and during the first World War, he worked in the Boston shipyards[1]. By 1920, Richard Derrick and his younger brother Marlin W. Derrick had made their way to the mining town of Terlingua where they both worked as store clerks[157]. At this time, the Derricks lived next to Wayne Cartledge and through this acquaintance, Cartledge knew of Richard Derrick's experience with machinery. In 1924, Cartledge hired Derrick to figure out the operation of the cotton gin and this led to Derrick's employment with La Harmonia.

Derrick moved from Terlingua to Santa Helena to work at the store, and that same year, 1924, he bought sections 15 and 16 of Block 16 GH&SA Railway Survey from Agapito Carrasco[5], the local *jefe* of El Ojito. He built his home on a site about three quarters of a mile southeast of the store. The Derrick house was a four room adobe structure built on a concrete floor with about 800 square feet of floor space. Part of the roof was covered with corrugated metal, and part was rolled roofing[8]. The house also had a screened porch that was 12 feet by 40 feet in size.

In 1944, the Big Bend National Park acquired the Richard Derrick house in a land transfer, and prior to 1964, the house was used as a ranger residence. In 1964, the Derrick house was occupied by Aaron and Wayne Green who patrolled this section of the Rio Grande as river riders, commonly known as "tick rid-

ers," for the U. S. Department of Agriculture Bureau of Animal Husbandry[8].

As the government acquired the land in the lower Big Bend for the national park, in 1942, there were about 4,000 acres of unpurchased park land at Castolon which belonged to the Cartledge family[1]. In 1957, Cartledge deeded the Castolon property to the National Park Service, but he retained the right to operate the store until 1960[68]. In 1961, the BBNP acquired the La Harmonia Company holdings and began operating the store as a concession[73]. The Castolon Historic District, also known as La Harmonia Ranch, Camp Santa Helena, and the Castolon Army Compound, was added to the National Register of Historic Places in 1974[46].

The Cartledge Legacy

Castolon, today, appears very much the way it was during the time of La Harmonia Company and its frontier store. The houses where Cartledge and the other company managers lived are occupied by the concessionaire employees, the other structures are still maintained and used for various service functions, and the store, still maintaining the La Harmonia name, provides the essentials of food and supplies to the locals and the park visitors. The park has permitted this enterprise to remain as a vestige of its former self and to become a living history exhibit for one of the most enduring examples of life in the Big Bend.

For nearly forty years, La Harmonia was the most important mercantile enterprise in this area of the Big Bend. The business proved to be most profitable when it provided hardware items, groceries, dry goods, medical needs, and farm and ranch supplies to Big Bend residents[1]. But, more than this, the company, under the guidance of Wayne Cartledge, worked to be a part of the community. Cartledge was instrumental in introducing a variety of agricultural products to the area including fruit trees, hogs, turkeys and bees[68]. Recognizing the need of the local residents to find ways to support themselves, he fashioned La Harmonia into a frontier trading post as well as a retail store. La Harmonia acted as a middleman for the Mexican fur trappers who brought their stocks of fox, beaver, wolf and bobcat pelts to the store to exchange for basic items such as groceries and general supplies[1]. The company also performed the role of wholesale distributor for the sale and shipment of locally produced candelilla wax[1], providing a source of income for the residents who harvested the desert plant and processed it into raw wax.

With an interest in the well being of the people that extended beyond mere business activities, Cartledge and La Harmonia served the Mexican and Mexican American population in other, more personal ways. Cartledge provided the residents of Castolon and the area with legal counsel. He assisted them in their business dealings and he helped them financially with loans. When the control of the border was tightened after the mid-1920's, Cartledge's records of the vital statistics of the community helped many of the local residents provide legal proof of their citizenship to U. S. Immigration officials[1].

When Cartledge arrived in the lower Big Bend in 1914, he found a society that was in transition. Anglo settlers had begun moving into the area in large numbers and they either displaced the Mexicans who were there or exploited them. By the 1920's, only a few of the original Mexican ranching families were still operating in the Big Bend[18]. Many Mexican Americans felt that they had been coerced into the sale of their land or cheated out of their ranches. The prejudice toward Mexicans and Mexican Americans was so common that one Brewster County lawyer described it thusly: "In this state, we have one set of laws for white people and one for Mexicans, all in the same words and in the same book[120]." At this time, too, the census records reflected the general Anglo sentiment in margin notes along side the entries for Mexican and Mexican American residents where it was written, somewhat derisively, "These are all Mexicans."

To his credit, Wayne Cartledge came to the lower Big Bend with an idea to mediate these and other contentious feelings in the community. He sought to have all of the people in the area live in a simple harmony. In his time with La Harmonia Company, Cartledge tried to live up to the ideal embodied in the name that he chose for his business. It is a fitting goal for residents and visitors of this valley of the Rio Grande, even today.

Santa Helena, Chihuahua, Mexico

Across the Rio Grande from Castolon is the village of Santa Helena. Unlike the similar instance of the "sister" villages of San Vicente, Texas and San Vicente, Coahuila in which the Texas community was established after the Mexican village had been in existence for several years, Santa Helena, Chihuahua was settled decades after Santa Helena was founded in Texas.

In 1935, Santa Elena was founded by thirty families from Juarez, near El Paso, who settled on the floodplain across from Castolon and established a cotton farming community. The success of La Harmonia's cotton farming may have been the motivation for such a relocation, but their timing was not very good. The venture was plagued with a drought and subsequent crop failures, and the town was abandoned a short time later[75].

In 1952, a second group of settlers from Juarez reestablished Santa Helena as an *ejido*, a communal farming organization. Nature was not kind to this venture either. A plague of insects descended on the crops in the fields and ruined their harvest. The misfortune caused the farmers of Santa Helena to abandon farming for ranching, and ranching remains the primary occupation of the villagers today. They raise cattle, horses, chickens, hogs and goats[75].

The village is situated on El Pista de Santa Helena, a trail dating from prehistoric times that connected the community of San Carlos with the Cerro Chino area[19]. Although the Sierra Ponce appears to be a formidable barrier, a traveler could cover the twenty-five miles over the Sierra Ponce to the modern Johnson Ranch in two days.

The village is named for its patron Saint Helen, the mother of the Roman Emperor Constantine and the person who, in 327 AD, was credited with discovery of the True Cross of Christ for which she was made a saint whose feast day is August 18[101].

Prior to the economic hardships caused by the closing of the informal border crossing at Santa Helena in May, 2002, Santa Helena was a thriving community of about 240 inhabitants. About fifty children, in grades one through six, attended the Jesus Alfredo Chavez Luna school, an adobe building with three classrooms. Religious services were held in the two churches in town, the Baptist Church and Santa Helena Catholic Church. And, visitors from the United States could take the ferry across to dine at one of three fine restaurants, Maria Elena's Restaurant, Enadina's (also known as La Frontera Restaurant) and El Canon Restaurant[75]. Today, the border is closed and crossing into Santa Helena is prohibited.

Rio Grande Village - Boquillas

The large campground complex of Rio Grande Village is the location of the earliest commercial center in what is now Big Bend National Park. From its beginnings, this community was part of the larger community of Boquillas that encompassed settlements on both sides of the Rio Grande. Although the river was a national boundary, it did not separate the two communities to the extent that they are legally and culturally divided today. Until the 1940's, the communities on each side of the river were named Boquillas, and for many years, especially in the decades around the end of the 19th century, they acted as an integrated community. The common denominator for the two Boquillas villages was the economic activity of the area, and that activity was based on mining.

Mexico has a long history of mining, and with the pacification of the northern frontier, mining activities began in the Sierra del Carmen of northern Coahuila, Mexico. Silver was discovered in the Sierra del Carmen at La Mina de la Fronteriza[1]. By 1883, lead and silver mines were opened in the mountains near what is now the village of Boquillas del Carmen[74]. This reflected a broader trend of the exploitation of mineral resources along the Rio Grande. The mining of silver began about 1885 in the Van Horn-Allamoore district of Hudspeth and Culbertson counties, and the mining of lead began about 1885 at the Presidio Mine in Presidio County as a by product of silver mining[145]. A decade later, in 1896, mercury mining started in the Terlingua district of Brewster County[145]. The Consolidated Kansas City Smelting and Refining Company, known as KSARCO, opened a smelter in El Paso, and the establishment of the railroad through Marathon made it feasible to transport the ore from Mexican mines to the processing plant.

The opening of the mines brought an influx of Mexican miners to the area, as well as others who worked in businesses supporting the mining operations. The Minas Ricas, about five miles from Boquillas del Carmen, was producing silver and lead by the mid-1890's, and soon investors from Texas joined with the Puerto Rico Mining Company to extract lead, zinc and silver ore from the mines and haul it to the railroad at Marathon[74]. By 1896, the population of Boquillas, Mexico was 1,000 persons[112]. A similar growth in population occurred on the Texas side where the estimate of the combined population of Boquillas, Texas and San Vicente, Texas was 300 people. On April 2, 1897, La Villa de Boquillas del Carmen was declared an official village by its first elected magistrate Federico Martinez[1].

The first permanent resident of Boquillas, Texas is considered to be Dennis Edward "Ed" Lindsey[143]. As a farmer from Mississippi[146], the young Lindsey recognized the potential of the broad floodplain of the Rio Grande in the area. In the early 1890's, he developed a small irrigated farm and established a store to supply food to the miners who worked in Mexico[2]. In 1894, the 32 year old Lindsey was appointed the U. S. Customs inspector, and he established a Customs Office at his home across the river from Boquillas, Mexico[143]. Lindsey's large white house, which still exists today, became the center of the community of Boquillas, Texas which grew up around it. Lindsey acted as the unofficial local postmaster of the village until an official post office was designated and he was appointed postmaster of Boquillas, TX on December 30, 1896[40].

Anticipating greater entrepreneurial opportunities, Lindsey graded a road from Marathon to Boquillas to support his store operations. He hired Mexican freighters to haul merchandise from the rail depot in Marathon to his store[1].

The Customs Station at Boquillas, the white building on the left, was originally established in 1894.

In 1897, KSARCO built a cable tram to transport the ore from Mexico to Texas where it had storage yards and a small smelter[44]. Lindsey's location near the end of the cable line was ideal for inspecting the ore shipments from Mexico[14]. KSARCO then upgraded Lindsey's road to a second class highway in order to get their equipment, supplies and laborers to the mining district[1]. Mexican freighters were operating 200 to 300 wagons to haul supplies to the mines. Their twelve mule wagons made regular trips in which they pulled 10,000 pound loads between Marathon and Boquillas[1].

In 1899, the American Smelting and Refining Company, known as ASARCO, took over the operation of the KSARCO tramway and the small processing plant it had constructed on the Texas side of the Rio Grande[143] near where the Barker Lodge is now located. Interestingly, Robert T. Hill, on his topographic survey of the Rio Grande in 1899, made note of the quarter mile long cable tram that linked the two villages of Boquillas, transporting silver ore to the United States for smelting and processing[1]. Hill also estimated the population of Boquillas, Mexico to be about 2,000 persons[143].

The economy of Boquillas was growing as never before and things seemed to be going very well for Lindsey, as well. He married his Mexican born wife Juanita in 1898, and they had their first child Jennie in December, 1899[146]. However, when some of the mines closed in 1900, Lindsey's business failed, and he closed his store[14]. While a downturn in the local economy may have contributed to his decision, his actions suggest that other factors may have influenced his behavior.

Prospecting fever was in the air. On October 10, 1902, Max Ernst advertised in the Alpine Avalanche a reward of nine weeks provisions from his store for the first discovery of cinnabar in the Boquillas area[14]. Martin Solis discovered the bright red mercury-bearing ore, cinnabar, near his ranch on the slopes of Mariscal Mountain[1]. Shortly thereafter, Ed Lindsay and William Harmon found cinnabar on the east side of Mariscal Mountain[14], and Lindsey filed the first mining claim on Mariscal Mountain. It is not known whether anyone collected the reward Ernst had offered, but both Solis and Lindsey had discovered cinnabar by November, 1903.

Realizing the importance of the discovery of cinnabar, Lindsey filed his claim and opened a mine[1]. The Lindsey Mine produced some ore, but the enterprise was beset with difficulties[82]. The cost of transporting the ore by mule the thirty miles to the smelter at Terlingua was very high. The site on Mariscal Mountain lacked water and lumber for the mine shafts had to be brought in. Lindsey also was involved in a lawsuit over the ownership of the property[82]. Ultimately, Lindsey gave up and closed the mine in August, 1904. In November, 1905, he sold his interest in the mine to Isaac Singer of Dallas, owner of the Texas Almaden Mining Company, who operated the mine until 1909[82]. Eventu-

ally, the Mariscal Mine became successful under W. K. Ellis who built the refining sections of the mine in 1916[3].

Ed Lindsey moved on to Lajitas to serve as the customs inspector there in 1904, and eventually, he wound up back in Marathon where, in 1910, he was working as a bartender in a saloon to support his large family. His wife Juanita died some time after the birth of their sixth child Ivey in 1921, and in 1930, the 57 year old widower was supporting the family by working as a farmer in the Marathon area[146].

An additional motive for Ed Lindsey's decision to close his Boquillas store and pursue other interests may have been competition from the other stores in the area. During the peak of the mining activity at the turn of the century, three other stores were operating in or near Boquillas. The Solis family, which owned Section 6 of Block 19, GC&SF Railway Survey, the site of the modern Rio Grande Village Campground, had established a store there about 1900. Martin Solis turned the operation of the store over to his son Benito when he moved to his new ranch near Mariscal Mountain. In addition, Jesse Deemer, a Boquillas resident since the early 1880's, was backed by Marathon merchant C. W. Hess in opening a store in Boquillas[143]. A third store was established by Max A. Ernst on land that he leased at the Big Tinaja waterhole which today is known as Ernst Tinaja.

Ernst had immigrated from Germany in September, 1873, at age 16. He became a U. S. citizen in 1890 while he was living in Alpine. In 1898, he leased section 66 of Block G2, a tract that included the Big Tinaja waterhole and a well that was known as La Noria ("the well")[14]. After purchasing the land at La Noria in 1901, Ernst actively promoted his La Noria community which is about eight miles north of Boquillas[143]. He ranched in the area, established a store which he called the Chisos Mountain Store[14], opened a school and served as a county commissioner, a notary public and the postmaster of Boquillas, Texas. Although Ernst was appointed postmaster of Boquillas, Texas on August 8, 1901, he declined the position[40]. However, in 1903, he successfully negotiated the relocation of the Boquillas post office to La Noria from its location near Boquillas Crossing[143]. The presence of the post office gave his store a competitive advantage over the other stores in the area, and his actions were most likely a source of friction between him and the other store owners, especially the Solis family.

On September 27, 1908, Max Ernst was ambushed as he rode through the gap in mountains on his return from Boquillas, Mexico to investigate a bad check sent through the mail at his post office[106]. The place of the shooting was on the sharp curve in the road leading out of the river valley above what is now Rio Grande Village. Today, the tunnel on the park road, built in 1959, bypasses the curve which was called Deadman's Curve after the Ernst killing[2].

Several members of the Solis family were among the twelve persons charged in the murder of Max Ernst, but, after three years of investigation, the murderer was not identified and no one was ever convicted of the crime[14]. Nevertheless, the episode devastated the Solis family, and in 1911, Benito Solis closed his store in Boquillas and moved away[143].

On December 10, 1908, James R. Landrum, a 33 year old lawyer from Florida who came to the area to recover from consumption, was appointed postmaster of Boquillas, Texas. Landrum, who was living in Alpine when Ernst was killed, was asked to be the executor of the estate[106] by Rosa Ernst, the widow whom Max had married only four years earlier[14]. Landrum moved to La Noria and operated the store until the estate could be settled. The estate of Max Ernst was closed in 1918, and Rosa Ernst took the cash assets from the estate valued at $13,751 and insurance of $5,000, remarried and moved to Nueces County. The property, which consisted of a store, a school building, about ten adobe cabins and several *jacales*, was sold to W. A. Weakley[14].

Around 1900, Carlos J. Moser promoted a plan to expand the mining operations in Boquillas. Moser, a German-born engineer from San Antonio, felt that it would be more profitable to transport large quantities of ore to the ASARCO smelter in El Paso than it was to process and refine the ore at the smaller smelter in Boquillas. As the president of the Del Carmen Mining Company[44], Moser organized the backing of several investors in Texas to construct a sophisticated aerial tramway and road system to haul ore from the Puerto Rico mine in the Sierra del Carmen to the rail depot in Marathon.

The centerpiece of Moser's plan was an aerial cable tramway that would span the Rio Grande and six miles of desert terrain in order to transport ore from the foothills in Mexico to a terminal on the high ridge of what is now Ernst Valley, 800 feet above the river floodplain. From the terminal, which was to be near the village of La Noria, a road was to be built to the Boquillas-Marathon Road permitting wagons to continue the transportation of the ore to Marathon. Moser's cable tram would consist of seventy-five wooden towers which carried ninety iron buckets of ore at a rate of seven and a half tons per hour[1]. This tramway would be built about two miles downstream from KSARCO's existing short tram.

Construction on the project began in 1907, and it would take three years to complete the aerial tramway system that was manufactured by the A. Leschen and Company of St. Louis[44]. In 1909, Moser hired Robert Farmer Jennings to oversee the construction of the ore road and the cable tram. The ore road was a seven and one third mile segment extending from the ore terminal up through Ernst Basin to the area near the Willow Tank Campsite where it joined Lindsey's Marathon-Boquillas Road which had been upgraded to a second class highway by ASARCO in 1897. Jennings, a 28 year old rancher from San Antonio, was the son of the well known cowboy Robert Jackson Jennings who rode on Chisholm Trail. He was ranching in Mexico at the time, and he set up his headquarters in Marathon to monitor the project and to assure delivery of the supplies to the construction site[44]. And, as the project neared completion in April, 1910, Moser himself was living in Marathon. The 52 year old Moser was staying at the hotel of John M. Chambers with his 29 year old wife Aimie whom he had married in 1908[149].

With the new tramway in operation, there was no need for the smelter in Boquillas. In 1911, KSARCO closed the Boquillas smelter and all of Mexican ore went to the rail line at Marathon via the tramway and wagons[143]. Farmer Jennings returned to ranching when the tramway was completed. When Carlos Moser died in 1915, his wife Aimee sold the tramway to the International Mining Company owned by F. C. Morehouse. Morehouse operated the Puerto Rico Mine and the aerial tramway until the mine closed shortly before the end of World War I in 1918[44].

Besides the completion of the tramway system, another reason that ASARCO abandoned the Boquillas smelter was the constant threat of banditry from northern Mexico. Revolutionaries allied with Pancho Villa, in addition to opportunistic bandits who capitalized on the chaos caused by the Villa Revolution, plundered the

Max Ernst was murdered as he rode through the pass along the road whose faint trace is visible on the hill from the tunnel.

Photo Credit: Louis F. Aulbach

The Ore Terminal in Ernst Valley lies in a collapsed ruin.

Big Bend regularly in the second decade of the 20th century. These outlaws would simply dash across the Rio Grande, strike their target and then return to Mexico with impunity.

The most noteworthy incident occurred on May 5, 1916 when a large group attacked the community at Glenn Springs. However, at the same time, a smaller group of bandits under former Villista Lt. Col. Natividad Alvarez crossed the Rio Grande at Boquillas and raided Jesse Deemer's general store. On that evening, Jesse Deemer and his supply clerk Monroe Payne, son of a former Black Seminole scout, were taken hostage[1]. In addition to Deemer and Payne, the bandits took eight employees of the aerial tramway company, the International Mining Company, captive[44]. Alvarez sent Deemer and Payne ahead into Mexico, while the other hostages were to be brought later by Alvarez and the rest of the outlaw band.

The miners working in the remote environment of Boquillas were an astute group, and before they had been transported more than a short distance into Mexico, the mine employees turned the tables on their captors. Alvarez was captured and was returned to Boquillas under guard[1].

In response to the raids, Colonel Frederick W. Sibley of the 14th Cavalry at Fort Clark was dispatched to Boquillas. Although the bandits had a three day head start, Sibley sent ahead a light force under Major George T. Langhorne, of the 8th Cavalry at El Paso, into Mexico in pursuit of the Mexican outlaws and their hostages. Langhorne, riding in his notorious Cadillac touring car, raced across the crossing at San Vicente and headed deep into the interior of Mexico. After about 200 miles, Langhorne and his troops were closing in on the renegades near the town of El Pino. With a dozen sharpshooters in his Cadillac, Langhorne entered the town. The bandits had dispersed, however, on the news of the arrival of the U. S. Army, and Deemer and Payne were found unharmed. Colonel Sibley and his troops re-entered Texas on May 21, 1916, and the episode known as the Second Punitive Expedition came to a successful end[1].

The events of the Boquillas raid had an unsettling effect on Jesse Deemer. Unwilling to risk the threat of bandits that persisted in subsequent years, Deemer closed his store in Boquillas and moved to California[143].

Although the unrest in Mexico was beginning to end by 1920, the mines in the area had closed, and the major economic activity of the Boquillas area became floodplain farming. In 1918, Jesus Estrada sold the tract that had previously been owned by the Solis family, Section 6 of Block G, to Swedish immigrant John O. Wedin. Wedin, who had farmed wheat in Kansas, installed an eight inch irrigation pump and a drainage system on his farm and successfully operated a wheat farm for about eight years[1]. Even today, campers at Rio Grande Village are familiar with the irrigation ditches that still bring water to the grassy areas of the campground

In 1926, John Wedin sold his land to Joe H. Graham of Del Rio, a rancher who had acquired the Buttrill ranch in the Rosillos Mountains in 1917. Graham's plan was to grow alfalfa and other grains to feed his cattle during the winter. Graham and his sons Frank and Jeff expanded the Wedin farm to the upstream section of the floodplain, and converted two adobe structures built by Wedin into a storage shed and a garage for their machinery[1].

The Depression brought financial difficulties to Joe Graham, and he lost the Rosillos Ranch and was forced to sell parts of his farm property. Graham sold one section to Texas state senator Benjamin F. Berkeley of Alpine who built the structure known as the Berkeley Cottage[1]. Berkeley called his retreat Ojos de Boquillas[120]. The upper section of the Graham farm was sold to John R. Daniels of Presidio in 1937[1].

In 1937, the Daniels family occupied the large structure built by Wedin and used by Graham for storage. The house is an adobe building with a vega and cane ceiling, an adobe roof and a flagstone floor[120]. Daniels enlarged the building to make a store, and his wife Mary ran the store to serve the local residents[1]. The Daniels Farm House and Complex, as it is known today, was headquarters of the John Daniels cotton farming operations. Although he was not a farmer by vocation, Daniels successfully practiced subsistence farming on his tract of 200 acres until about 1942[1]. The Daniels Farm House was added to the National Register of Historic Places in 1989[46].

For a decade during the 1920's and 1930's, the most popular place to dine in the Boquillas area was Chata's Place. Maria G. "Chata" Sada and her husband Juan owned a combination trading post, general store, cafe and hotel at Boquillas. Chata ran the store in Texas while Juan operated a silver mine in the Sierra del Carmen.

Chata Sada was born on December 4, 1884 in Iraxuato, Mexico, and Juan Sada was born in Nueva Leon in 1870. Both Juan and Chata arrived in the Boquillas area in the 1880's and the two were married in 1901 at Boquillas, Coahuila[14], where they opened a general merchandise store and saloon. In 1926, the Sada family immigrated to the United States and established a general store and cafe in Boquillas, Texas. They had no children of their own, but they "adopted" many of the local children and took them into their care[14]. Chata's Place served as the unofficial community center for both villages on the river. After Juan Sada died in 1936, Chata moved to Del Rio to live with one of her adopted sons. Chata Sada died there on July 13, 1973[14].

On October 27, 1933, Texas Governor Miriam Ferguson signed a bill that set aside land near Santa Elena Canyon, Mariscal Canyon and Boquillas Canyon for the proposed Texas Canyons State Park[1]. That was the beginning of the process that led to the creation of the Big Bend National Park a decade later. From the late 1930's until the 1950's, the population of Boquillas, Texas ranged from twenty-five to forty people. By the early 1960's, its population declined to six people as the park developed the area into Rio Grande Village. Today, Rio Grande Village is probably the most heavily utilized area of the park, but nearly all of the residents are transient campground guests.

In the same way that Boquillas, Texas had depended on the mines of Boquillas, Coahuila for its economic existence in the early 1900's, by the start of this century, Boquillas del Carmen, Coahuila had become dependent on the tourism from Big Bend National Park as the basis of its economy. In 2000, about twenty-five families lived in the village which had two churches, Santa Maria del Carmen and a Baptist Church, Falcon's Restaurant, and the Buzzard's Roost Bed and Breakfast offering rooms and meals to the tourists. However, after the closing of the unofficial, but historically used, border crossings at Boquillas and San Vicente in May, 2002, the economy of the Mexican village deteriorated significantly. After an eleven year wait, the border crossing at Boquillas reopened on April 10, 2013. It remains to be seen how long it will take for the community of Boquillas to rebound.

Photo Credit: Louis F. Aulbach

Although Chata's place was demolished by the park, the faint ruins of the house can be seen across the road from the former customs station. A small cemetery lies behind the site where a handful of graves remain. One prominent grave is that for "Julio" who passed away in 1940. Perhaps this one of Chata's adopted sons.

A few of the ore tramway towers, with the original steel cables, are still standing, although in a much deteriorated condition.

La Linda, Coahuila, Mexico

The end of a Boquillas Canyon trip is at the gravel bar below the bridge to La Linda. This take out is also the point of beginning for a trip through the Lower Canyons of the Rio Grande.

Besides the bridge, the most prominent feature of the area is the flourspar plant on the high bank on the Mexican side of the Rio Grande. The plant was constructed by the Dow Chemical Company in the early 1960's to exploit the rich deposits of fluorspar located in the nearby mountains of Mexico[114]. The bridge, called the Gerstacker Bridge after an official of the company, was built in 1964 by Dow Chemical to facilitate the transport of fluorspar from the mines at La Linda to Marathon. Trucks carrying the ore crossed the bridge and took the paved road to the railroad terminal at Marathon[37].

The village of La Linda developed in support of the plant and it had about four hundred residents during the time the plant was operational. By 1990, over 3.5 million cubic tons of fluoride was mined from La Linda's Cuatros Palmos and Aguachile mines. However, when China was granted most favored nation trading privileges in 1990, the La Linda mining operation was no longer profitable. China's fluorspar could be delivered to processors for $100 per ton while cost of the La Linda ore was $125 per ton. The DuPont Corporation, which had purchased the plant from Dow Chemical, closed the facility[114].

The La Linda bridge was barricaded and closed in 1998 after a Mexican customs inspector was killed at the bridge. For a while, a company of the Mexican cavalry was stationed near the La Linda bridge to patrol the roads upstream for gun runners and others who were transporting electronics, drugs and other contraband in both directions across the Rio Grande[114].

For a while after the closing of the bridge, trucks continued to use the historic Tom Heath cattle crossing located about 1,000 feet downstream of the bridge[114]. Thomas B. Heath was born in Texas in February, 1876, and by 1900, he was a rancher working out of Marathon. His exploits in the area are now only recalled by the nearby canyon which bears his name, and by 1920, Heath had settled down and had become a cotton farmer in Medina County[115].

The Minera de Musquiz acquired the La Linda mines by 2002, but ore is shipped into Mexico, not across the bridge. The plant remains idle, yet it is believed that the 1 to 2 million tons of mineral tailings at La Linda, which contain fluorine, beryllium and arsenic, may be economically valuable if the prices for those minerals rise. The village of La Linda, today, is mostly deserted, yet the picturesque little church on the outskirts of town appears to continue to serve the residents of the area[85].

The National Parks Conservation Association took ownership of the La Linda bridge from the DuPont Corporation in expectation that they could transfer it to the National Park Service, however, the unsettled political situation along the border has put that option on hold. Efforts by local officials to save the bridge from destruction have resulted in it being renamed the Hallie Stillwell Memorial Bridge[114].

Andy Kurie, owner of the Heath Canyon Ranch, worked as a geologist for both Dow and DuPont at La Linda. Kurie bought the housing that DuPont had constructed on the Texas side of the river, and he refurbished it into tourist cabins[114]. For a number of years, Kurie operated the Heath Canyon Guest Ranch, but he has now retired to his home in El Paso. His ranch foremen, Fred, however, maintains the property and provides river access and parking for a fee for those paddling the Rio Grande.

Terlingua Creek

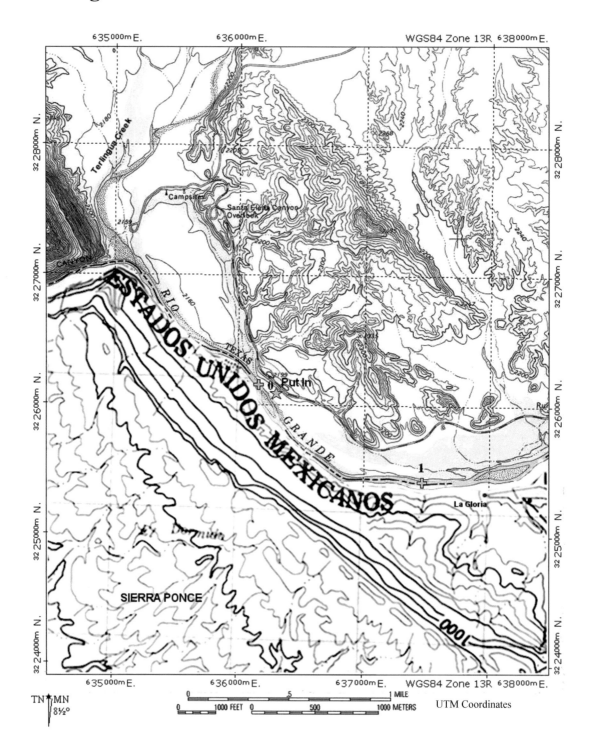

Mile   Description

Santa Elena Canyon. As perhaps the best known feature of the Rio Grande in Big Bend National Park, this "textbook" canyon was called the Great Canon San Carlos in the 18th and 19th centuries[120], but it appeared on the 1904 USGS topographic map as the Grand Canyon of Santa Helena[125]. The name had been anglicized to Santa Elena in Park publications by the late 1950's.

Terlingua Creek (TX). As early as 1855, United States maps showed this drainage as Lates Lengua Creek[125]. County survey maps and field survey notes by John T. Gano, a Presidio County surveyor of the 1880's, recorded the creek variously as Tos Linguas and Tasa Linguas Arroyo, suggesting that a corruption of the native pronunciation was taking place[124]. On the 1884 Military Map of Texas, it became Tarlingua Creek[125], and when the local mining district was established in the late 1890's, the name was standardized on the modern spelling as Terlingua.

In the 1880's, Mexican families drifted into the area along Terlingua Creek and the Rio Grande, tending goats and farming the land along the Rio Grande. These immigrants provided fresh vegetables and a supply of labor to the Americans who were beginning to establish ranches in the Big Bend. They established a small village on Terlingua Creek about two miles above the Rio Grande and called it Terlingua[63]. When the larger community grew up around the Chisos Mine farther upstream, the Mexican community assumed the name **Terlingua Abaja**, or Lower Terlingua, about 1903[1].

When the mines began operating, Mexican teamsters with wagons and mules found work with the mines hauling wood, supplies and the flasks of mercury to Marfa. By 1905, Paz Molinar and his brothers Juan and Vicente, who owned property near Terlingua Abaja called Rancho Molinar[1], were prominent freighters and contractors for the mines. They established the **Molinar Community** on the west bank of Terlingua Creek, near Rattlesnake Mountain, on a road from Terlingua to the farming communities near what is now Castolon[5].

0   **Put in at the Santa Elena Take Out / Terlingua Creek access.**

1   **La Gloria, Mexico.** - "the glory" - Mexican soldiers manned this isolated military outpost around 1918. Today, you might see a local rancher and his truck there.

Photo Credit: Terry Burgess

The Santa Elena Access sometimes is a nice gravel bar, as seen above. At other times, the river cuts close to the bank, and the access to the river is not so convenient.

Alamo Creek

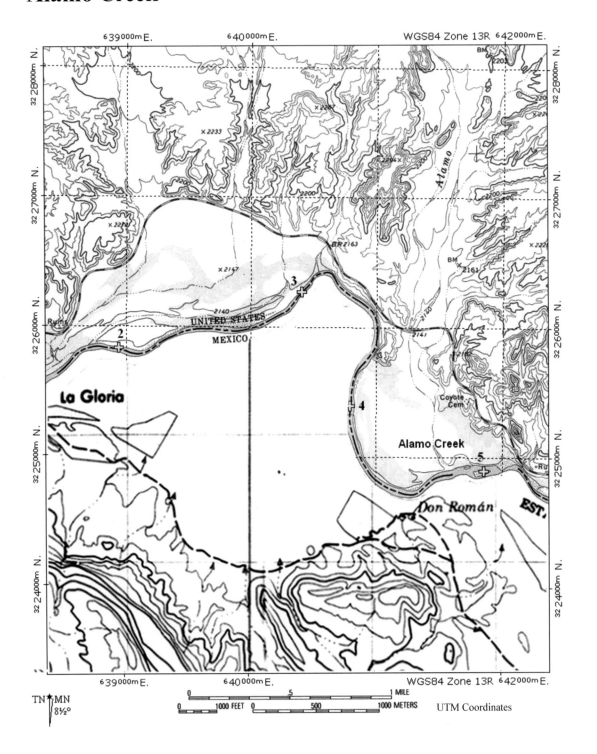

Mile	Description

1   **Dorgan-Sublett Complex.** In 1918, James Sublett bought the C. E. Metcalf homestead, which Metcalf had filed on in 1915 and proved for title in three years. Sublett and Albert W. Dorgan then formed a partnership to irrigate and farm the floodplain[1]. Sublett converted the old Metcalf house into a store and he hired Alvino Ybarra and Cisto Avila, local stone masons, to build him a home on top of the hill and a smaller house for his farmhands below it[1]. Dorgan and his wife lived in a three room rock and adobe house built across an arroyo to the southwest[2].

About a decade after moving to the area, Albert Dorgan supervised the construction of an elaborate house on the hill about 3/4 mile northeast of the Sublett house. The most interesting feature of the Dorgan house was the large living room with its spectacular two-way fireplace made of elegant native stone[2]. Albert Dorgan remained in the area until the early 1940's when their land was acquired for the Big Bend National Park[39].

3   **Creek (TX).** A short, unnamed arroyo drains the upland gravel terrace.

4   **Don Roman, Mexico.** A small community overlooking the floodplain on the Mexican side.

Alamo Creek (TX) - "poplar, cottonwood" - Although the area at the confluence of Alamo Creek and the Rio Grande appears barren and forbidding today, it was a veritable oasis in the desert in the 19th century. In 1852, 2Lt. Duff C. Green, leader of the U. S. Army escort for the boundary survey crew through the area, noted that this open area a few miles below Santa Elena Canyon was well timbered and suitable for cultivation. He marked it as a potential site for a military post[1]. In 1860, Col. Robert E. Lee, commander of the Army in Texas, ordered 2Lt. William Echols to locate a site for a fort on the Rio Grande near the Comanche Trail[1]. On July 26, 1860, Lt. Echols found the site about four miles downstream from the Grande Puerta, previously identified by Green, which had plenty of timber and an abundance of grass. Echols decided that the site was the best place to build a post since it had a fine valley on each side of the river for cultivation to supply the post and any adjacent settlements, it had moderately elevated gravel mesas for building locations, and there was plenty of grazing for animals. Furthermore, Echols noted that the Mexican population was anxious for the establishment of the post which they could supply with corn, fruits and vegetables just as they did from San Carlos and Presidio to Fort Davis[117].

La Coyota Cemetery (TX). This cemetery served the community of La Coyota from about 1903 to 1942. Relatives of the persons buried here still visit and care for the final resting places of their kin. Please be respectful when you visit.

The magnificent stone chimney is only one facet of the Dorgan House that shows the innovative ways that man has adapted to the harsh environment of the lower Big Bend.

Albert Dorgan built this house in the late 1920's and lived in it until the early 1940's.

Photo Credit: Dana Enos

Castolon

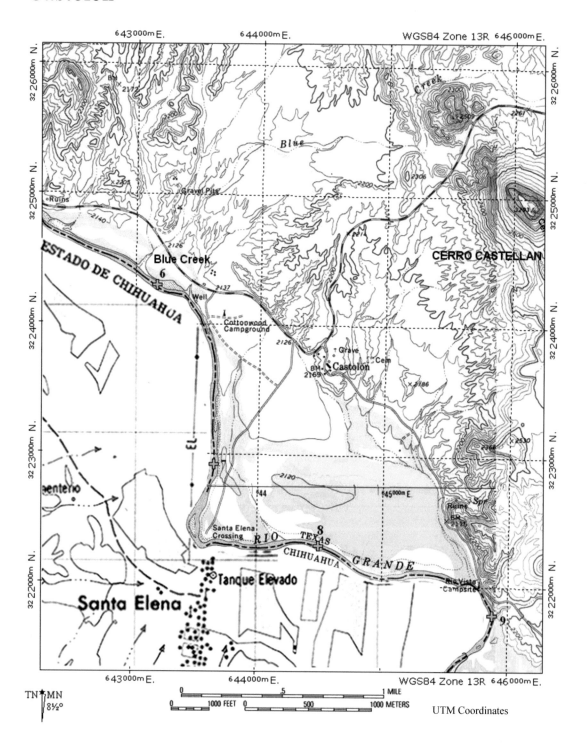

| Mile | Description |

5 **La Coyota, Texas.** In 1908, Ruperto Chavarria led a group of about nine families of immigrants to the west bank of Alamo Creek and this settlement which they called La Coyota[1] when an early settler killed a coyote that was trying to break into a hen house[161]. The La Coyota community practiced subsistence farming in the floodplain, raising corn, beans, wheat, tomatoes, squash and melons. Many of them also worked on the Sublett farm. Others cut and hauled wood for the mines at Terlingua[2]. The community prospered along with the mines near Terlingua and it declined as the mining operations ended.

Blue Creek (TX). This creek descends from high in the Chisos Mountains near Laguna Meadows and it is a major drainage in the Castolon area. Archeological evidence suggests that the creek has been inhabited for thousands of years[66]. Homer Wilson established his Blue Creek Ranch along the upper stretches of the creek in the foothills of the Chisos Mountains in 1929, and he operated it until his death in July, 1943. His widow turned over their land to the state for the park in early 1945[159].

6 **Cottonwood Campground (BBNP).** This is one of the developed campgrounds in the Park. It is located adjacent to the site of the La Harmonia Company cotton gin and across the road from the restored site of the La Harmonia Store from about 1914 to 1921. The campground is in a grove of large cottonwood trees that had been planted by the Park since 1954 to demonstrate the stands of timber that existed in the area prior to the cutting of the trees during the period of mining operations in Terlingua. A NOAA stream flow gauge is located in the Rio Grande near the entrance to the campground.

The two story, adobe cotton gin and pump house was built by Wayne Cartledge in 1922. The cotton gin was permanently abandoned in 1929, but the pump house continued to be used for irrigation until 1942. The BBNP acquired the cotton gin in 1961. It still housed its rusting machinery in 1964, but during a record flood in 1974, the remains of the cotton gin and its heavy machinery were washed downstream[2]. The ruins of the 60 ft by 55 ft foundation are visible near the entry road to the campground[8].

7 **Santa Elena, Mexico.** This small village was originally established in 1935 by thirty families from Juarez[75]. Travel to the village from the park is not permitted since the informal border crossings are currently closed. More information is available on page 25.

Castolon, Texas. Originally called Santa Helena, this community has been the predominant business and social center of the area since the late 1890's. See the related discussion on page 14.

8 **El Ojito, Texas.** - "the little spring" - Shortly after Cipriano Hernandez came to the area (now known as Castolon) in 1903, Agapito Carrasco settled six Mexican families at a community he called El Ojito, about a mile downstream of Hernandez[68]. It was one in a string of subsistence farming communities along the river that also included Santa Helena (Castolon), La Coyota, Terlingua Abaja, the Molinar Community and Buenos Aires.

Rio Vista Campsite (BBNP) - closed. This campground was closed in 1975 after a large flood washed out the River Road along the bluff downstream of the campground[3]. The road was re-routed near the Buenos Aires Primitive Campsite to go north of Cerro Castellan. Remnants of the old road are still visible from the river.

Photo Credit: Louis F. Aulbach

The Castolon Cemetery has approximately 70 graves which gives us an idea of the large population that lived in the area.

Las Congojas

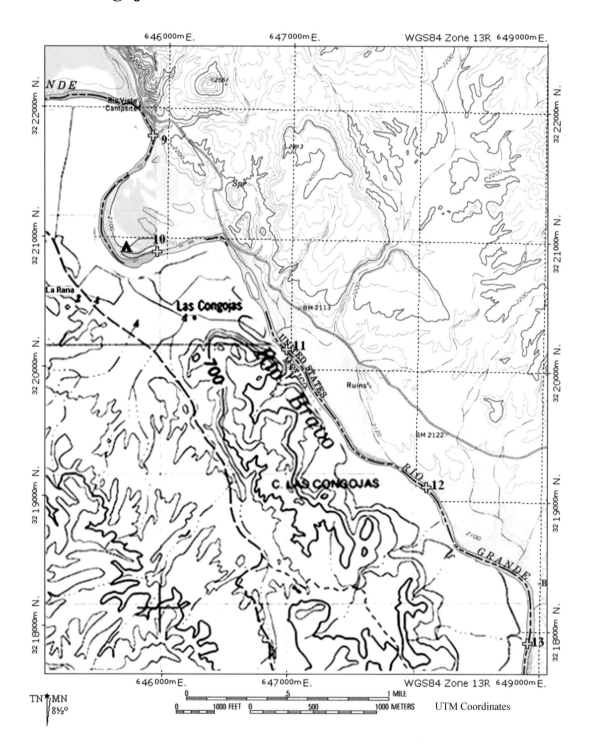

Mile   Description

9   **La Rana, Mexico.** - "the frog" - A small ranching community.

10   **Las Congojas, Mexico** - "the worries or the anxieties" - A small ranching community that may have gotten its name from the time when the community was part of the military colony defenses against the marauding Apaches and Comanches that were based in San Carlos.

11   **Smuggler's Canyon (TX).** This narrow canyon has been known as Smuggler's Canyon since in the early days of the Park. Mexican nationals carrying contraband could slip back across the river through this canyon without being detected[3]. In a small drainage, about a mile north of Smuggler's Canyon are the ruins of the Roman De la O Ranch. The 17 year old De la O immigrated in 1883 and worked as a teamster near Terlingua. About 1911, he established his rancheria in Section 18[163] near a spring which provided a good water supply. He built his house of rock and used the box canyon of the side wash to maintain his livestock. His cattle fed on the abundant chino grass which grew on the surrounding hills[3]. In late spring or early summer of 1917, Roman De la O, age 51, was ambushed near Smuggler's Canyon, killed and thrown in the river. His widow moved the family to Alpine and sold the property to Faustino Pineda in October, 1917[163]. The ruins of the De la O Ranch are north of the River Road about 100 yards into a small box canyon which has a spring identified by the presence of large cottonwood trees[3]. One of the two graves on the hill south of the house may be De la O's final resting place.

Buenos Aires Campsite (BBNP). One of the Primitive Backcountry Campsites in BBNP. The USGS Topo map still shows the old route of the River Road, but the current route turns north at the campsite and goes north of the ridge that contains Smuggler's Canyon.

Photo Credit: Louis F. Aulbach

The De la O Ranch was located in this small box canyon about a mile north of Smuggler's Canyon (right). The large cottonwood trees indicate the presence of a good spring.

The large gravel bar in the sweeping bend near Mile 10 makes a good "first night" camp (below). Camping is prohibited in Texas, and discouraged in Mexico, from the end of the Santa Elena Canyon nature trail to ¾ mile downstream of Castolon.

Photo Credit: Terry Burgess

Smoky Creek

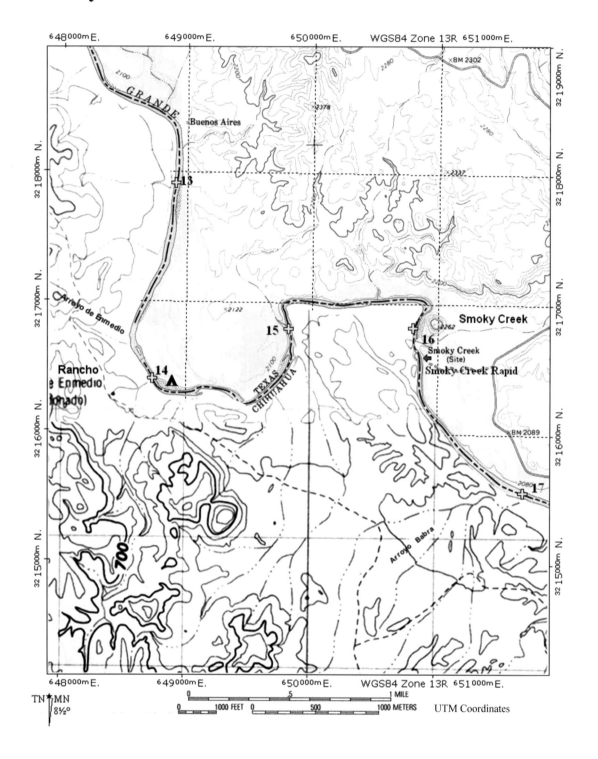

TN   MN
8½°

UTM Coordinates

Mile   Description

12   **Buenos Aires, Texas.** The residents of this Mexican settlement farmed the floodplain during the 1920's and 1930's, raising frijoles, corn, pumpkins and feed for goats and livestock[3]. The community consisted of a handful of small rock houses on the side of a hill overlooking a sharp southerly bend of the Rio Grande. One house is remarkable for its finely crafted rock fireplace and chimney.

13   **Arroyo de Enmedio (Mex).**

           Rancho de Enmedio, Mexico.

16   **Smoky Creek (TX).** This creek is a major drainage on the south side of the Chisos Mountains. A prominent formation identifies your approach to the outlet of the creek.

           Smoky Creek Rapid, Class I-II.

           Arroyo el Abra (Mex) - "it opens"

Photo Credit: Louis F. Aulbach

The ruins of the Buenos Aires community are located on a bluff overlooking the Rio Grande (left). From this vantage point, looking upstream, the low hills in the foreground are Cerro Las Congojas while the Sierra Ponce dominates the background.

The isolated butte rising from the floodplain (right) signals that you are approaching Smoky Creek. The Smoky Creek community site is located on the south side of the butte. A small rapid is usually found in low water, downstream of the junction with Smoky Creek.

Photo Credit: Louis F. Aulbach

Black Dike

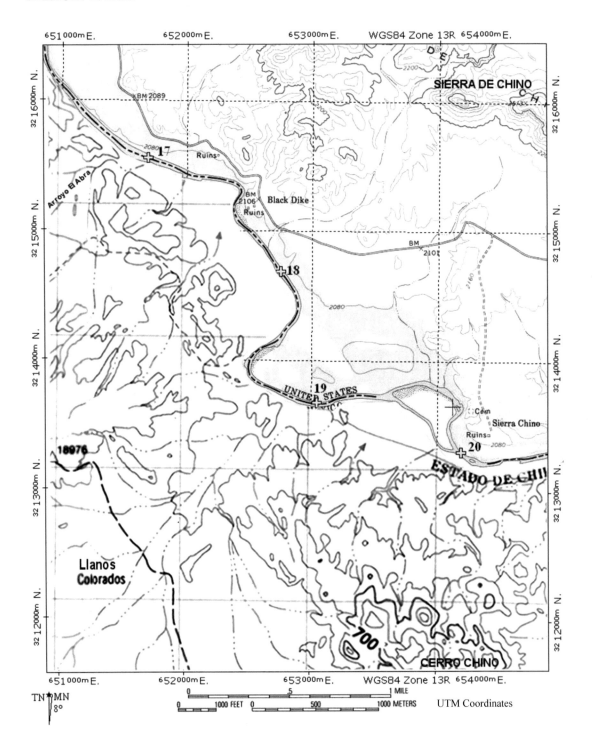

SIERRA DE CHINO

BM 2089

17   Ruins

Arroyo El Abra

BM
2106   Black Dike
Ruins

BM
2107

13

2080

UNITED STATES   19
MEXICO

Cem
Sierra Chino
Ruins
20

18976

ESTADO DE CHI

Llanos
Colorados

700

CERRO CHINO

651000mE.   652000mE.   653000mE.   WGS84 Zone 13R   654000mE.

32 16000m N.   32 15000m N.   32 14000m N.   32 13000m N.   32 12000m N.

TN   MN
8°

0   5   1 MILE
0   1000 FEET   0   500   1000 METERS   UTM Coordinates

Mile   Description

17   **Black Dike.** One of the many radial dikes that run out from the Punta de la Sierra[3]. The volcanic activity that thrust up the Chisos Mountains fractured the sedimentary limestone and allowed molten lava to fill the fissures. The lava cooled and hardened in the fissures, and when the softer sedimentary rocks eroded away, the harder ridges of lava remained to form the dikes[118]. Black Dike is exposed by the river and it cuts into the Rio Grande. Extending almost completely across the river, the dike creates a good fishing hole.

Black Dike Campsite (BBNP). This Primitive Backcountry Campsite is located on the floodplain near the site of the Black Dike community. The residents farmed small plots and grew wheat. The threshing circle where the wheat was processed is visible near the River Road. Goat raisers in the village built little kidhouses, or *chiquiteros*, for their young goats. The kids were tethered to a stake with a small rope near the kidhouse so that they would stay in the shade while the nanny goat grazed during the day[3].

19   **Creek (Mex).**

Sierra Chino, Texas. Sierra Chino is named for the heavy growth of chino grass that grew in the area. Chino grass is the Mexican name for the abundant, curly grama grass, *Bouteloua ap*, that is excellent forage for horses and cattle at all seasons of the year[39]. Since both sides of the river have a "Chino Mountain," the grass must have been abundant on both sides of the river. Today, the area is a fishing camp.

These canoes are tied up to the volcanic formation of hard, dark rock known as the Black Dike. Unable to erode through or penetrate the Black Dike, the river makes a 90 degree turn along the face of the formation. Looking downstream, the Sierra Ponce is in the background.

Photo Credit: Terry Burgess

Gauging Station

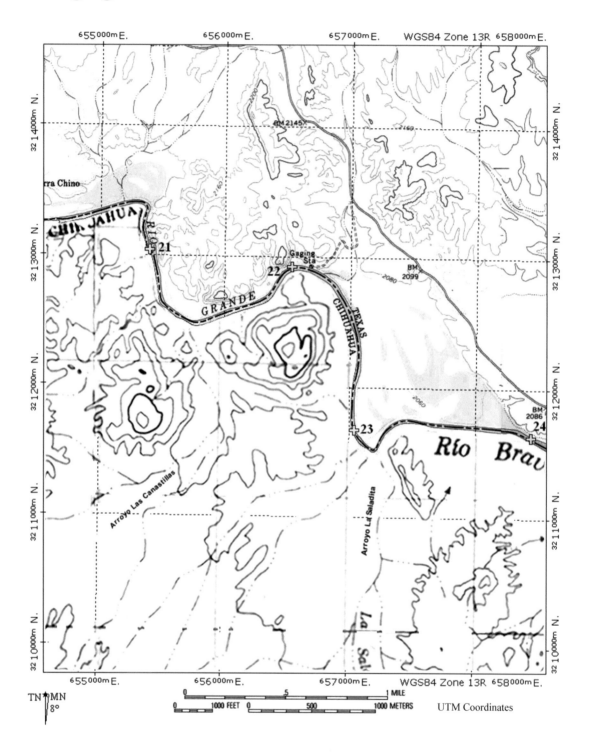

Mile   Description

21   Arroyo Las Canastillas (Mex) - "the baskets"

22   IBWC Gauging Station (TX). The Gauging Station was establish on April 1, 1936 by the International Boundary and Water Commission to measure the flow of the Rio Grande[3]. A Primitive Backcountry Campsite is located near the Gauging Station. The place is regarded as a good fishing hole.

23   Arroyo La Saladita (Mex).

Photo Credit: Louis F. Aulbach

The Johnson Ranch Gauging Station is located in this small canyon.

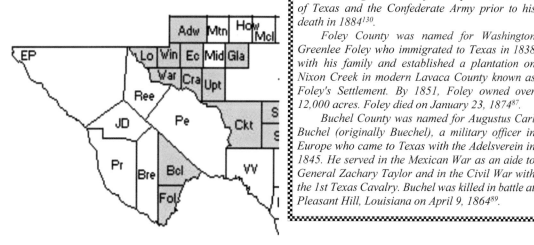

This sketch of Texas counties in 1887 shows the location of Buchel County (Bcl) and Foley County (Fol) in relation to Brewster County (Bre).

A little known fact...

At one time, what is now Brewster County was actually three counties. Brewster County was only the western half of the modern county. The eastern half was divided between Foley County and Buchel County. The boundary line between Foley County and Brewster County met the Rio Grande just east of the Gauging Station site[90].

Foley County was formed from Presidio County on March 15, 1887 along with Buchel County and Jeff Davis County shortly after a similar act created Brewster County out of part of Presidio County. Buchel and Foley Counties were never organized, and on March 22, 1889[88], they were attached to Brewster County for judicial and surveying purposes. Foley County and Buchel County were abolished by the state legislature on April 9, 1897 when they were added to Brewster County[91].

Brewster County, the largest county in Texas, was named for Henry P. Brewster[129]. Brewster arrived in Texas on April 2, 1836 and fought at the Battle of San Jacinto, and later, he practiced law, served in the government of the Republic, the State of Texas and the Confederate Army prior to his death in 1884[130].

Foley County was named for Washington Greenlee Foley who immigrated to Texas in 1838 with his family and established a plantation on Nixon Creek in modern Lavaca County known as Foley's Settlement. By 1851, Foley owned over 12,000 acres. Foley died on January 23, 1874[87].

Buchel County was named for Augustus Carl Buchel (originally Buechel), a military officer in Europe who came to Texas with the Adelsverein in 1845. He served in the Mexican War as an aide to General Zachary Taylor and in the Civil War with the 1st Texas Cavalry. Buchel was killed in battle at Pleasant Hill, Louisiana on April 9, 1864[89].

Johnson Ranch

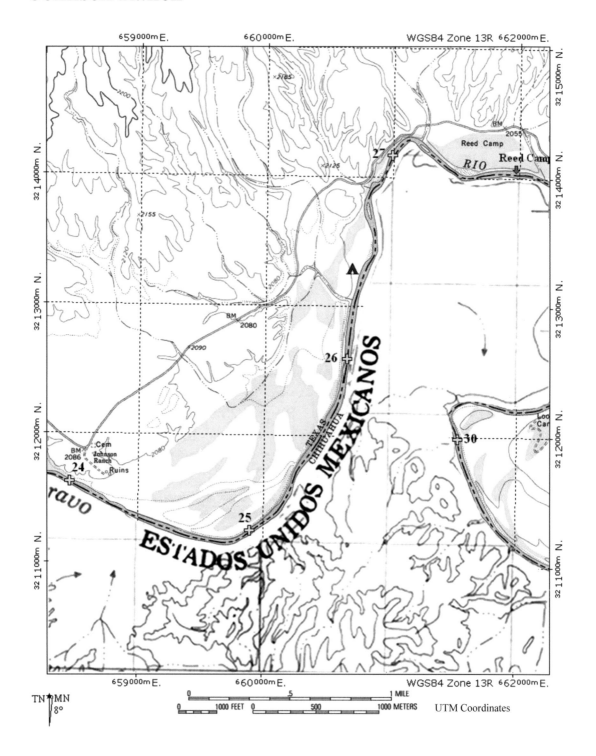

TN MN
8°

UTM Coordinates

| Mile | Description |

24   **Johnson Ranch (TX).** By 1924, partners George N. Graddy and William P. Williams were living on the land east of the modern Gauging Station[6]. Williams, age 68 and divorced, had come from Kentucky and, by 1920, was lodging in Alpine where he worked as a trapper and rancher[132]. Graddy, a 28 year old farmer from Kentucky, joined Williams in homesteading along the Rio Grande. In August, 1928, when Williams and Graddy had gained title to the land, they sold the property to Elmo Johnson[1]. By 1930, Graddy, although unemployed, was living in San Antonio with his wife Mable[131]. Williams had bought and was operating a poultry farm in Alpine[132].

Elmo Johnson had farmed in North Texas for several years, but in 1928, he and his wife Ada moved into the house on the Big Bend property and established a trading post[1]. They were joined there by their friend Wilfred Dudley "W. D." Smithers, a photographer and journalist for the San Antonio newspaper[1]. On April 11, 1929, a band of thirty armed Mexican revolutionary soldiers came to the ranch in search of food and medicine and took away Johnson's goats and cattle. Realizing the need for military protection during the unrest associated with the Escobar Revolution[73], W. D. Smithers immediately appealed to his friend Col. Arthur G. Fisher, the commander of the 8th Air Corps at Fort Sam Houston in San Antonio. Smithers convinced Fisher that the Johnson Ranch would make a good emergency landing field[1].

Smithers returned from San Antonio with a truckload of oil, gas, tires and supplies to service the airplanes. Johnson borrowed a road grader from the county and proceeded to make a landing strip on the gravel terrace above the floodplain near their home[1].

On April 24, 1929, within two weeks of the raid, Lt. Thad V. Foster flew a De Havilland DH-4 to the Johnson Ranch and made the first landing at the airfield. Foster flew in and made the first entry in the field register which was subsequently maintained on the patio of the Johnson home. He also brought the official authorization of the Johnson Ranch airfield that the War Department leased for $1 per year. The airfield was the first permanent installation of the Air Corps in the lower Big Bend, and it held a strategic position for combat troops during the border emergencies[81].

During the next several years, W. D. Smithers used his residence at the Johnson Ranch as the base for his documentation of the culture of Mexican Americans in the Big Bend[65]. With the help of local workers, including five Mexican families who lived across the river[16], Elmo Johnson operated a trading post, a cotton farm and a goat ranch in addition to maintaining the airfield[3]. By 1932, the airfield had three graded runways, the longest of which was 4,200 feet[81].

The peak of activity at the Johnson Ranch airfield was during 1936. During 1940, there were only two flights to the airfield. In 1943, the airfield ceased operations, and Johnson sold his property for the park[81].

The ruin of the Johnson Ranch house is the largest adobe ruin in Big Bend National Park[3]. The **Johnson Ranch Campsite (BBNP)** is a Primitive Backcountry Campsite that is located on the floodplain directly below the foundations of the ranch house. Out buildings for the ranch and the airfield are visible near the River Road where it passes near the ranch house. Upon careful inspection, traces of the three runways can be seen. A cemetery is also located on the site.

26   **Creek (TX).**

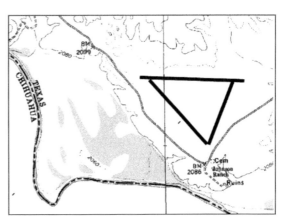

The location of the three runways of the Johnson Ranch Airfield are shown in the drawing.

Reed Camp

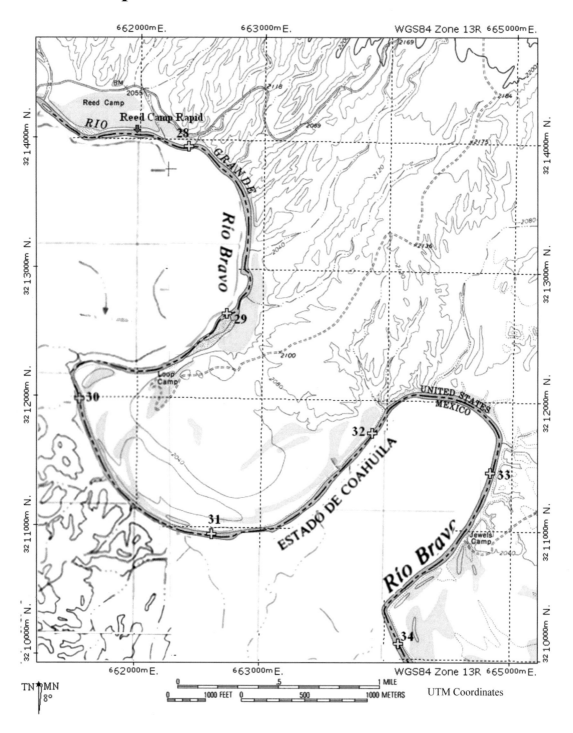

Mile   Description

27   **Punta de la Sierra (TX).** Magnificent views of the southern edge of the Chisos Mountains dominate the
         skyline as you approach the turn toward Reed Camp. The Punta de la Sierra's serrated outline is formed from
         hard lava. Five bands of black rock in the ridge of the Punta de la Sierra show that the volcanic activity of
         the Chisos Mountains covered the area with lava flows five different times. The wedge shaped mass of lava
         at the end of the ridge of the Punta de la Sierra suggests that it was one of the fissures through which the lava
         reached the surface[118].

         Reed Camp, Texas. This fishing camp may be named for the notorious Alvin and Virginia Reed family[14]
         who lived at various places in the lower Big Bend during the late 19th and early 20th centuries. Various
         members of this family were involved in illegal or violent activities at various times. In 1930, ranchers named
         Holguin and Garcia lived in the area[6].

         Reed Camp Rapid. Class II.

29   **Loop Camp (BBNP).** This Primitive Backcountry Campsite was named for the its location at the base of the
         long loop made by the meandering course of the Rio Grande[3]. Pablo Baiza was living in the area around
         1930[6].

31   **Adobe ruins (Mex).** The ruins visible above the Mexican bank may be the ruins of the military outpost of
         Santa Helena[160]. Elmo Johnson spoke of the ruins that may have been built in conjunction with the military
         colonies established to defend the northern frontier from Apache and Comanche raids[16].

33   **Jewel's Camp (BBNP).** The origin of the name for this Primitive Backcountry Campsite is not known,
         however, there is some speculation that the name refers to Jewel Wilson Babb, wife of Walter Babb[34] of the
         Babb family[84] which owned extensive holdings in Trans Pecos and the Big Bend[32] during the first half of the
         20th century. She, later, was famous as the "border healing woman[33]." Jewel Babb died in Valentine, TX in
         1991 at age 90[35].

Photo Credit: Louis F. Aulbach

*Each time the river takes a northerly course in the several miles downstream of Johnson's Ranch, the dramatic relief of Punta de
la Sierra fills the skyline. Note, too, in this picture the thick growth of river cane along the banks. The Rio Grande meanders for
several miles in this area and the cane makes access to the uplands difficult, at best. Be alert for good campsites well ahead of
time.*

Woodsons

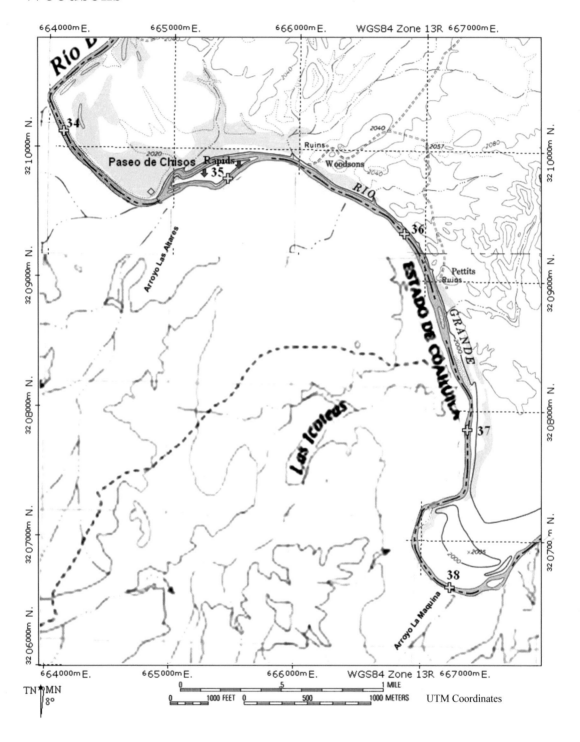

664000m E.   665000m E.   666000m E.   WGS84 Zone 13R 667000m E.

Río D

34

2020
Paseo de Chisos   Rapids

35

Ruins
Woodsons   2040
2057   2080
2040

RIO

36

Pettits
Ruins

Arroyo Las Altares

ESTADO DE COAHUILA

GRANDE

Las Icoleas

2000

37

x2035
2000

38

Arroyo La Maquina

32 10000m N.
32 09000m N.
32 08000m N.
32 07000m N.
32 06000m N.

664000m E.   665000m E.   666000m E.   WGS84 Zone 13R 667000m E.

TN MN
8°

0   5   1 MILE
0   1000 FEET 0   500   1000 METERS

UTM Coordinates

| Mile | Description |

34 **Arroyo Los Altares (Mex).** - "the altars" - The outwash of this large drainage creates a braided stream of gravel bars and islands in the Rio Grande. This area has historically[125] been called the **Paseo de Chisos**[1] (or sometimes Paso del Chisos[107]), and it is thought to be the river crossing of the main route of the eastern branch[123] of the **Great Comanche Trail**[2]. The community of Altares, about 30 miles south of the Rio Grande, is a settlement that dates from about 1805[77]. The boundary between Mexican states of Chihuahua and Coahuila[105] is located near the point where Arroyo Los Altares joins the Rio Grande.

Creek (TX).

Paseo de Chisos Rapid. Class II.

35 **Creek (TX).**

Woodson's Campsite (BBNP). This Primitive Backcountry Campsite was named for John Woodson[53] who ranched in the area during the late 1920's and 1930's. In the 1890's, Santiago Baisa ran cattle along the Rio Grande in this area[1]. Woodson's is considered one of the best fishing holes in the BBNP as the sandstones ledges allow easy fishing from the bank[3]. These ledges contain bedrock mortar holes indicating that native Americans have also used the site extensively[123].

36 **Pettits, Texas.** In 1910, J. N. Pettit, 54 years old, owned a stock ranch in Presidio County which he ran with his son S. Harvey Pettit[95]. The 26 year old Harvey lived on the ranch with his wife Ora, 24, and their daughter Viola, 2. By 1920, Harvey Pettit and his family, which now included son Clifton who was born in 1911, had bought a ranch in Brewster County near Dug Out and John W. Rice at Chilicotal Spring[53]. The Pettit's continued to live on the ranch near Dug Out[95] into the 1930's, and it is unclear how the site on the Rio Grande became associated with their name. However, by 1930, Henry D. Glasscock, a 43 year old Texas Ranger who had come to the area from Del Rio, was homesteading the site with his 22 year old wife Pearl whom he married in 1929[133]. It is presumed that the abandoned automobiles at the site are his.

Arroyo Las Icoteas (Mex).

38 **Arroyo La Maquina (Mex).** - "the machine"

Photo Credit: Louis F. Aulbach

Looking north from a hill near the mouth of Arroyo Los Altares in Mexico, you can see Talley Mountain in the center-right of the picture and Chilicotal Mountain in the distance. The Comanche Trail came right over the saddle to the left of Talley Mountain and crossed the Rio Grande near this place, Paseo de Chisos.

Arroyo Las Garzas

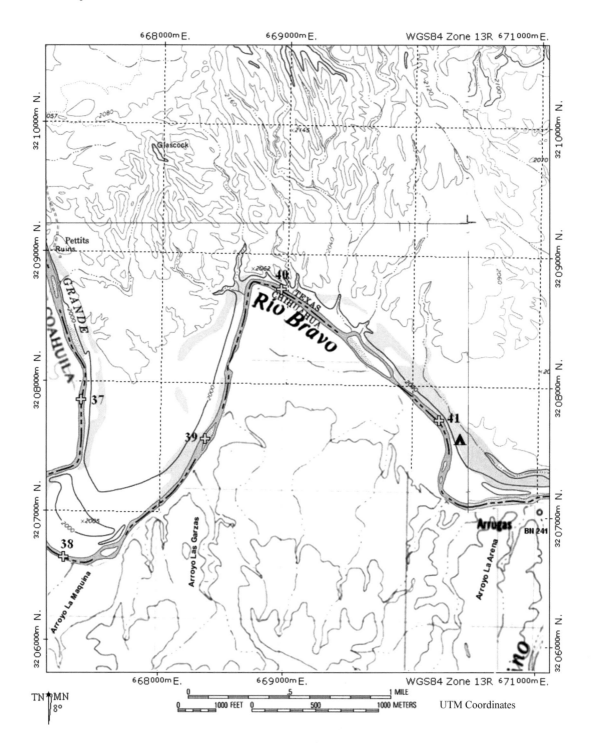

UTM Coordinates

Mile   Description

38   **Arroyo Las Garzas (Mex).** - "the herons"

39   **Creek (TX).** This creek drains the slopes of Glascock Mountain, a small hill named for 1930's settler Henry D. Glasscock, a Texas Ranger who homesteaded the site known as Pettits[133].

40   **Creek (TX).**

41   **Campsite (TX).** A good campsite can be found at the upper end of the grassy sandbar.

           Campsite (Mex). There is a good campsite near the mouth of Arroyo La Arena where the river turns east at the base of a small bluff.

           Arroyo La Arena (Mex). - "the sand"

           Arrugas, Mexico. - "wrinkles"

A little known fact...

The Great Comanche War Trail went south from the Fort Stockton area and separated into two main branches in the Big Bend area. The western branch crossed the Rio Grande at Lajitas and continued on to San Carlos (modern Manuel Benavides), Chihuahua, Mexico[160]. The eastern branch followed Tornillo Creek south before bifurcating. One fork went to San Vicente, Coahuila, Mexico[1], while the other fork, which was often referred to as the "main branch[120]," entered the foothills of the Chisos Mountains en route to the Glenn Springs area before crossing the Rio Grande at the Paseo de Chisos, an area of shallows near the modern Woodson's site[123].

Photo Credit: Terry Burgess

As the river turns to the north below Arroyo Las Garzas, the South Rim of the Chisos Mountains and Elephant Tusk Mountain (formerly Indianola Peak) are quite apparent on the horizon.

Santa Fe del Pino

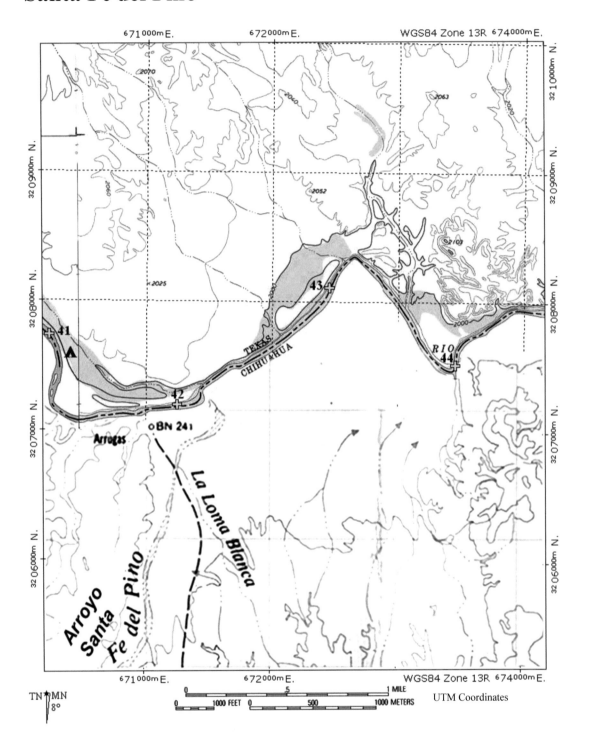

Mile	Description

42   **Arroyo Santa Fe del Pino (Mex).** - "the holy faith of the pine" - About 1930, Frederico Diablo lived in Texas across the river from Arroyo Santa Fe del Pino[6].

Creek (TX).

Arroyo La Loma Blanca (Mex) - "the white hill" - This creek joins Arroyo Santa Fe del Pino just a short distance above the confluence with the Rio Grande.

43   **Creek (TX).**

Creek (TX) - This creek drains the slopes of Cow Heaven Mountain. John and Mary Potter[104] operated a ranch in the valley during the 1920's and 1930's. Cow Heaven Mountain was named because of the large stands of chino grass that grew in the area before the land was ruined by overgrazing[118]. After that, the story was that Cow Heaven Mountain got its name from a local rancher who observed that the land was so barren that a cow would have to go to heaven if she was stranded on it because there was no grass to eat[120].

44   **Creek (Mex).**

A little known fact...

The Mariscal Mine, on the north flank of Mariscal Mountain (below), produced only a small percentage of the mercury extracted from the mines in the Big Bend region. The Chisos Mine at Terlingua was by far the largest producer[62], however, the Mariscal Mine stands today as the finest example of the mercury mining industry in Texas. The remoteness of its location has allowed the mine to remain largely intact, showcasing the various stages of its development and the construction of state of the art facilities[1] prior to the closure of the mine in 1943[82].

Photo Credit: Louis F. Aulbach

The ruins of the Mariscal Mine.

Talley

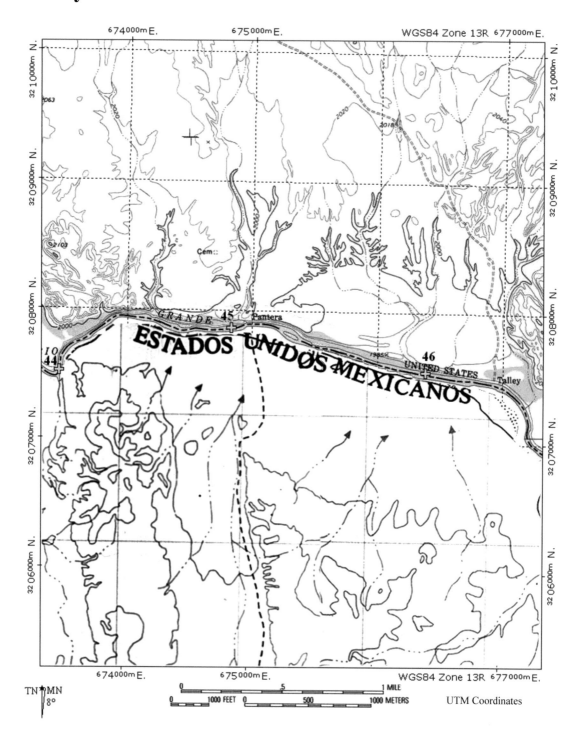

TN MN
8°

0   5   1 MILE
0   1000 FEET   0   500   1000 METERS

UTM Coordinates

Mile   Description

44   **Creek (TX).**

45   **Creek (TX).**

46   **Pantera, Texas** - "the panther" - A primitive road comes to the river on the Mexican bank opposite the Pantera site. It is not uncommon to see Mexicans who have driven to this point.

Talley, Texas. J. M. Talley moved to the area in 1902 and built a home near the river for his wife and two children[3]. He farmed the floodplain and raised goats. Then, in 1909, Talley sold his farm to J. R. Walker[3] who had come to Texas from Missouri in the 1880's[53].

In 1930, J. R. Walker was a widower, and, at age 75, he and his 43 year old son Det Walker[6] worked the ranch[53]. Although the Walkers lived in the area for more than 30 years, until the 1940's, the place has always been known as Talley.

The ruins of the Talley Ranch house are on the bank of the Rio Grande, near the end of the road[3].

Put in. Trips through Mariscal Canyon use the Talley site as a put in, often to take out at Solis Landing. The road to Talley can be long and difficult. Check the BBNP Road Conditions Report before making plans to access the river here.

Photo Credit: Terry Burgess

Shortly after leaving Talley, the river enters into the heart of Mariscal Mountain. The canyon walls rise above you and the narrow slot of the canyon is awe inspiring.

Mariscal Canyon

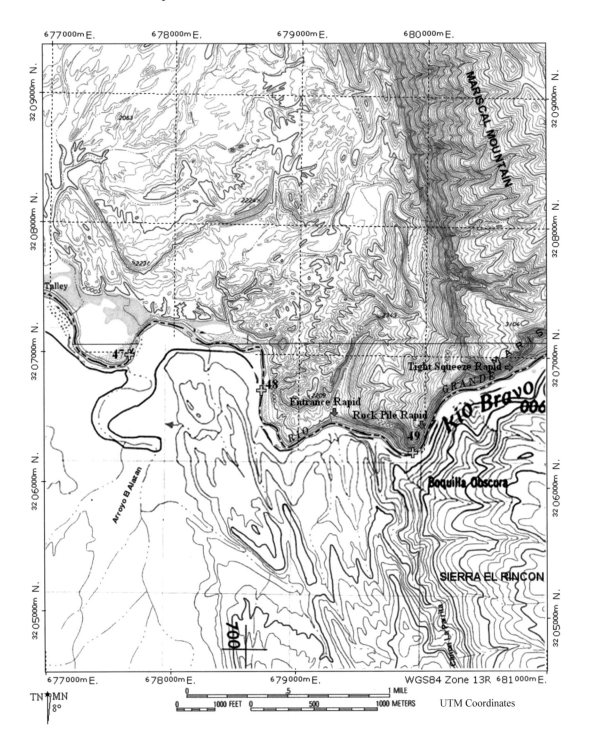

Mile   Description

47   **Arroyo El Alazan (Mex)** - "the sorrel horse" - Shortly after leaving Talley, the river enters the flanks of
           Mariscal Mountain. Within a short time, and after several short bends, you will find yourself deep within
           the canyon and the flow picks up speed.

           Creek (TX).

48   **Entrance Rapid. Class I-II.** This is the first rapid within the canyon, however, it usually is not more than a
           riffle.

           Canon La Parrita (Mex). The "Big Bend" of the Rio Grande occurs near the mouth of this arroyo[56]. The
           river makes its southernmost descent at this point before curving up and away from the low point of the bend.

49   **Rock Pile Rapid. Class II.** Although the name of this rapid conjures up thoughts of its namesake in Santa
           Elena Canyon, this rapid can be negotiated with much less difficulty. Although it can require some
           maneuvering, the rapid can usually be run without scouting.

           Tight Squeeze Rapid. Class II-III. This is the most difficult rapid in the canyon. There is a large gravel bar
           on the Mexican side where you can pull out well above the rapid. Scout the approach and the run from the
           boulders on the Mexican side.

Photo Credit: Louis F. Aulbach

Jack Richardson runs the Rock Pile Rapid in his 20 foot XL Tripper. At this level, about 4 feet on the Johnson Gauge, the route through the rocks is easily discerned.

The relative size of the boulders and the slot in the Tight Squeeze can be seen as Natalie Wiest negotiates the narrow passage flawlessly. The water level on the Johnson Gauge was about 4.2 feet.

Photo Credit: Louis F. Aulbach

Cross Canyons

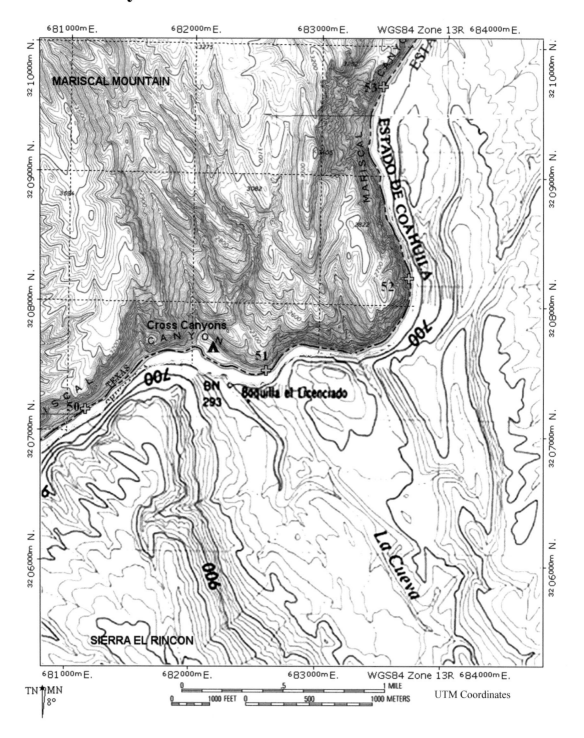

Mile   Description

50   **Cross Canyons (TX).** There is a large outwash at the mouth of this canyon that provides a large and, usually grassy, camping area. It is a good pace for a layover day, since the hiking on both sides of the river is spectacular.

Arroyo La Cueva (Mex) - "the cave" - "You can recognize a couple of turtles and some other animals." With that statement in the early 1970's, Bob Burleson, president of the Texas Explorer's Club, one of the earliest canoe expedition and adventure organizations in Texas, recorded the petroglyphs of Mariscal Canyon, perhaps for the first time[37]. There are actually two panels on adjacent boulders. The second panel of petroglyphs appears to be more abstract and geometric in form which may indicate that they date from a different, and possible earlier, period.

Of the two petroglyph panels in Arroyo La Cueva, this panel contains figures that are easily recognizable as animals of the area. The turtle is particularly distinct, while the other figures appear to be either a centipede or a scorpion. The lowest figure may be a snail. Take a good look yourself and see what you think.

The second panel (not pictured) contains more abstract and geometric art, and it has mortar holes in the rock.

The Cross Canyon site is a large campsite that can accommodate a large group, and it makes a good spot for a lay over day since there are excellent hikes on both the Texas side and the Mexican side of the river.

Solis

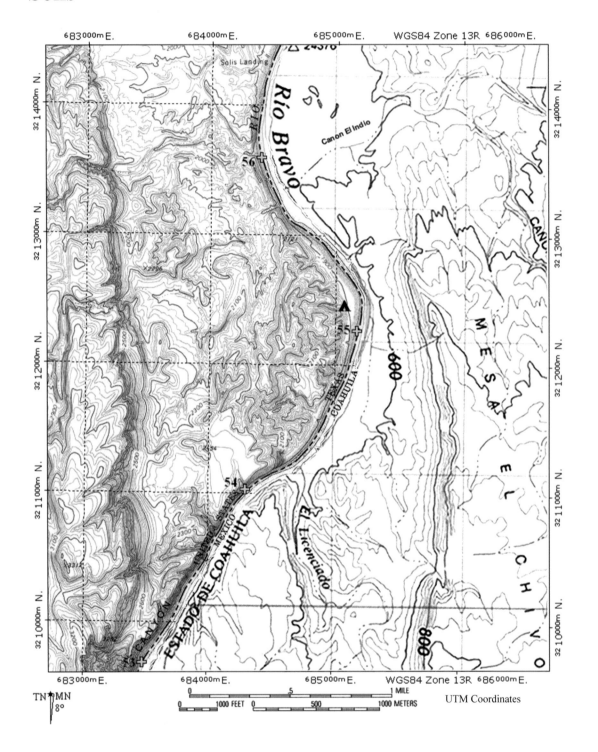

TN MN
8°

UTM Coordinates

Mile   Description

54   Arroyo El Licenciado (Mex) - "the lawyer"

55   Canon El Indio (Mex) - "the Indian"

Solis Landing (TX). The landing is a take out point for short trips through Mariscal Canyon.

Solis Campsite (BBNP). This is a Primitive Backcountry Campsite located in the vicinity of the landing.

Solis Landing is merely a cut in the river cane along the bank. The thick growth of the cane makes it difficult to see the opening. If this is your take out, be alert.

Photo Credit: Louis F. Aulbach

A little known fact...

Around 1890, a number of ranchers from the San Carlos area moved into the Big Bend area of Texas. Attracted by the chino grass and other native grasses in the area, these Mexicans built homes and established ranches across the border in Texas at about the same time as Texans were beginning to settle on ranches there as well. Among the most prominent of these early Mexican ranchers were Felix Dominguez, Felix Gomez, Ramon Molinar and Martin Solis and his sons[18].

Martin Solis, born in January, 1840 in Mexico, immigrated to Texas about 1875 with his wife Juanita whom he married in 1870, and his sons and extended family. The Solis family was in the Boquillas, Texas area by 1890. In March, 1893, he registered his brand at the county courthouse in Alpine. In 1894, Solis applied for a lease on Sections 6 and 8, Block G19 GC&SF Railway Survey. He homesteaded on section 6, and he built a house and a store near the river at what is now the Rio Grande Village Campground[14].

In an effort to expand his prosperous operations, Martin Solis bought land on the eastern slope of Mariscal Mountain from James Dawson in 1897[14]. The land had plenty of grass and water and better grazing for the horse ranch he had established. Solis built a home on section 3, Block 18 GC&SF Railway Survey[14], near modern Casa de Piedra site[7], and turned over the store near Boquillas to son Benito[14].

On September 5, 1898, Juan, Tomas and Benito Solis each separately registered brands for their horse and cattle ranch. Martin Solis and youngest son Francisco used the previously registered brand. By 1900, Martin Solis had substantial property holdings[14], and the Solis ranch extended along the Rio Grande from east of Mariscal Mountain and north to Glenn Spring. For the better part of a decade or more, the Solis Ranch supplied beef to the mining communities along the river[1] and cattle and horses to the local ranchers[14].

The Solis family rode large, but nimble, horses that seemed to complement the aristocratic demeanor of the elder Solis. Martin Solis, a wiry, light, Roman-nosed man, was proud of his Spanish ancestry[14]. He made some claims that he was a descendent of Juan de Solis, the discoverer of Paraguay[14], and may have been related to Gaspar Jose de Solis, who led an inspection of the Texas missions in 1767, and other famous members of the Solis family. Martin Solis was an excellent horseman, and the fact that he could read and write both English and Spanish[14], gave credence to his claim of noble origins.

(Continued on page 65)

Fresno Creek

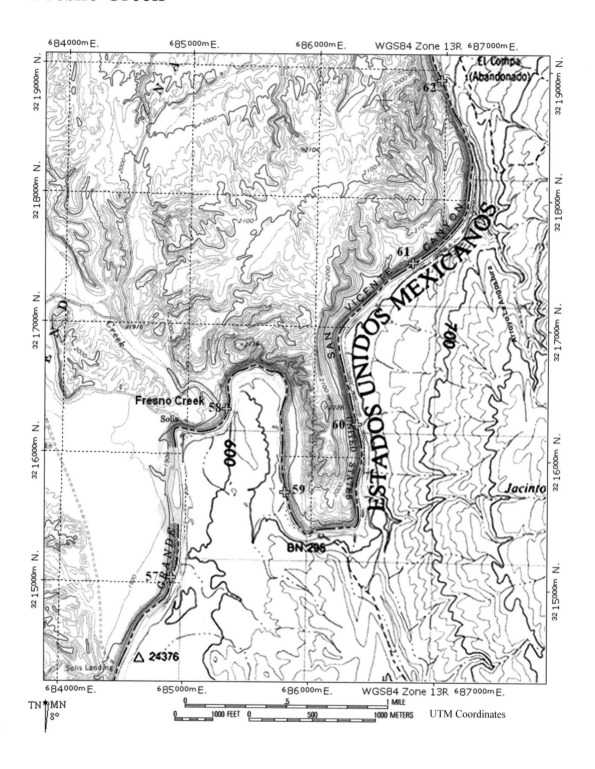

TN↑MN
8°

1000 FEET

1000 METERS

UTM Coordinates

Mile	Description

57   **Solis, Texas.** The Solis family ranched the land east of Mariscal Mountain and north to Glenn Spring from 1900 to 1926. From 1926 to the early 1950's, others farmed the flat lands of the Solis area until the land was purchased for the park. Situated between Mariscal Mountain and Sierra San Vicente, the Solis area is a geological formation called a graben (German for grave). At the end of the Cretaceous Period, geologic activity resulted in this large block of land dropping down or sinking to create the graben[3].

   Fresno Creek (TX) - "ash"

59   **Arroyo Jacinto (Mex)** - "hyacinth"

   San Vicente Canyon

61   **Arroyo La Angostura (Mex)** - "the narrowness"

The Solis Brand.

(Continued from page 63)   *The distinguished and remarkable Solis brand, a stylized Spanish brand[107] in the form of an "F" with a flowing cap, an angled cross hash and a backswept foot, seemed completely appropriate for "Don Martin" and his family's extensive ranching operations.*

In 1905, Francisco Solis married Pabla Salmon and they moved to San Vicente, Texas. Tomas Solis married Felisa Ureta in January, 1906, and they moved to the family's Boquillas store where the other sons had established a small family compound[14]. Benito Solis, who was 34 in 1906, worked the store as a merchant selling goods[110]. He lived with his wife, two sons and two daughters next to his brother Tomas. Tomas, 33, was married and had two sons. He worked as a rancher and lived next to Juan. Juan, the oldest son at 35, was a rancher and lived nearby with his wife Doroteia, his son and four daughters. By 1910, Francisco, his wife and two sons had moved to the family property near Boquillas where he worked as a laborer doing odd jobs[110].

In 1908, an incident occurred that had a devastating effect on the Solis family of the Big Bend. On September 27, 1908, Max Ernst, the owner of the Chisos Mountain Store in La Noria and prominent member of the community, was shot three times with a .44 caliber Winchester rifle, ambushed as he rode through the gap in mountains on his return from Boquillas, Mexico to investigate a fraudulent check sent through mail at his post office[106]. Before he died, Ernst wrote a note indicating he thought one of the Solis family shot him[3].

In October, 1908, the Grand Jury of Brewster County charged Francisco, Tomas, Juan, Benito and Martin Solis and seven others with the murder of Max Ernst on a complaint made by Rosa Ernst who knew of trouble between her husband and the Solis family[14]. The case was dismissed on March 18, 1909, and all of the charges were dropped for lack of evidence[3]. The murderer of Max Ernst was never found, but, the murder accusations left a tremendous cloud over the Solis family. The Solis family ultimately sold their holdings in the Big Bend and moved away[14]. Martin died about 1910, and his widow had moved to El Paso by the time the documents from the sale of some of his land was completed in 1911[14].

Benito ranched the the Glenn Spring area after the death of his father, but on February 18, 1916, he sold his land at Glenn Springs to W. K. Ellis[14]. The Solis land on section 6, Block G19 passed between the Solis sons Tomas and Benito before it was finally sold for taxes in the early 1920's[14]. The headquarters of the Solis Ranch near Mariscal Mountain was sold by Martin's grandson Ygnacio Solis to J. G. Estrada in May, 1926[14].

From 1926 to the early 1950's, others settlers farmed the floodplain of the Solis area until the land was purchased for the park. Today, there remains a single grave site on the Solis Ranch[17]. On the west side of the road, near the top of a low ridge, there is a simple grave piled with stones. It is not known who is buried there. Perhaps it is someone who settled in the area at a later time. Yet, the lonely grave and the solitary resting place seem to be a fitting tribute to the man who gave his name to the area, Don Martin Solis.

Comptons

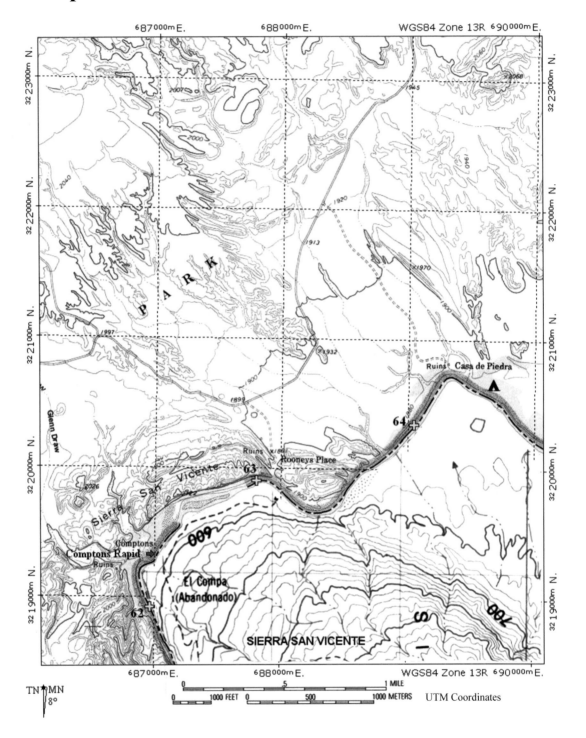

Mile   Description

62   **Sierra San Vicente (Mex).** About 140 million years ago, during the Mesozoic Era, geologic forces caused the arching of the rock strata that is Sierra San Vicente. This large anticlinal fold has been eroded so that the soft layers on top have been removed to expose the massive limestone that forms its crest[3].

El Campa, Mexico - "it stands out"

Glenn Draw (TX). This drainage begins with flows from Juniper Canyon in the Chisos Mountains and forms its main canyon near Glenn Spring in the foothills of the Chisos Mountains to the south of Chilicotal Mountain. Glenn Spring, with its reliable water source, was a primary camping stop on eastern branch of the Great Comanche Trail. Evidence of native American occupation includes flint debris, mortar holes and pictographs. In the 1880's, the first Anglo settler in the area, H. E. Glenn, had a remuda of horses in the area. He dug out and walled the largest spring for a better supply of water, but he was killed by Indians near the spring[80].

In 1914, Captain C. D. Wood and W. K. Ellis established a candelilla wax factory near the spring to use the plentiful water to exploit the abundance of the wax plant in the area. The factory employed 40 to 60 Mexican workers[80]. On the night of May 5, 1916, several armed Mexicans under Captain Rodriguez Ramirez attacked the community at Glenn Springs. Four people were killed, four were severely wounded, the store looted, two major buildings were partially burned and the wax factory destroyed, never to reopen[80].

Today, the Glenn Springs site consists of the foundations of the factory and the large house. The Mexican community of Glenn Springs, on the west side of Glenn Draw near the spring[80], can be seen in the ruins of a few rock houses. Its cemetery of about thirteen graves is on an adjoining hill, and it is still visited and maintained by the relatives of those buried.

Compton's, Texas. This location was a popular fishing camp on the river bank just north of where Glenn Draw joins the Rio Grande[3]. C. G. Compton was hired by Wood and Ellis in 1914 to run the general store and post office at Glenn Springs where they had established a candelilla wax factory.

Compton's Rapid. Class II.

63   **Rooney's Place, Texas.** This is the site of the ruins of a river front rock house which belonged to the Rooney family. Francis Rooney, born about 1868, came to Texas from Ireland in 1880 and grew up near Ft Stockton[14]. He became a naturalized citizen in 1890, and in 1894, he married the 16 year old Seleta Martha Chambers in Marathon[86]. Rooney, one of the pioneer ranchers of Brewster County, registered one of the early cattle brands of the county on July 19, 1895[92]. Throughout his long career, he owned and operated ranches through out Brewster County.

In 1900, the 33 year old Rooney had a ranch in the Chisos Mountains where he lived with his wife Leta, 22, daughter Katherine S., 2, and sons John Monroe, 4, and Francis P, 8 months. Rooney was working a ranch near Marathon in 1910, and the family had grown to include son Walter, born in 1903, and daughter Margaret Ann, born in 1910[93].

The Rooney boys followed their father into the ranching business. By 1920, John M. Rooney, age 24, was a rancher himself in the Marathon area, and the younger Francis, Jr., a 20 year old, worked as a ranch cowboy[93]. During the 1930's, the elder Rooney, now in his 60's, lived at the Lightning Ranch, one of the smaller ranches near Marathon that was bought out by the Gage Ranch[107]. In 1945, Francis Rooney died at age 77[86].

64   **Casa de Piedra, Texas** - "house of rock" - possibly the ruins of the headquarters of the Martin Solis Ranch, circa 1898 - 1926[14].

San Vicente

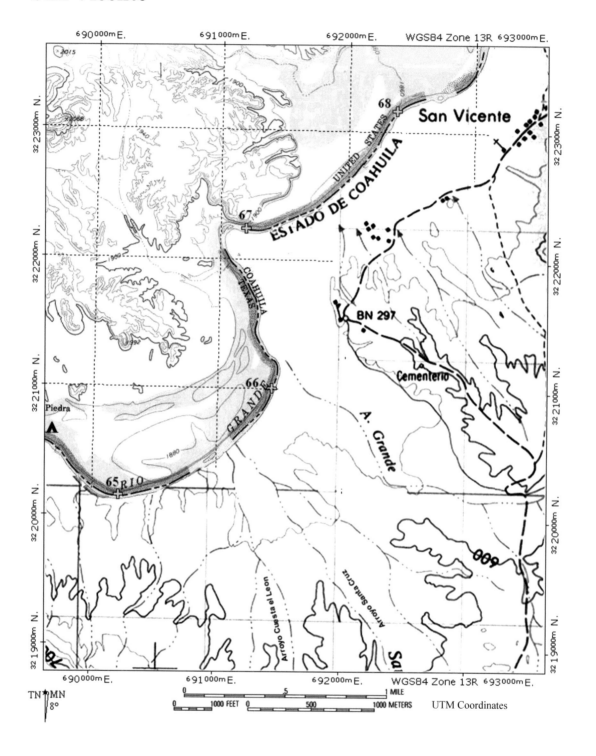

Mile   Description

65   **Arroyo Cuesta el Leon (Mex)** - "the hill of the lion"

           Arroyo Santa Cruz (Mex) - "Holy Cross"

66   **Arroyo Grande (Mex)** - "big"

Presidio San Vicente, Mexico. The migration of the Apache southward from the southern Great Plains to the Big Bend and northern Mexico began about 1650. For well over a century the Apache, whose name is derived from the Zuni word *Apachu* meaning *enemy*, inhabited the Gran Apacheria and harassed the settlements of northern Mexico[1].

In late 1772, Colonel Hugo de O'Conor, commandant inspector of all military forces on the northern frontier, selected a site for the presidio at San Vicente at the point of entry into northern Mexico of the Lipan and Mescalero Apaches[1]. Although lacking in wood and forage, the graveled plateau overlooking the Rio Grande was high enough to serve as an observation post and offered a strategic advantage for O'Conor's San Vicente presidio. In order to accommodate the presidio structure to the irregular shape of the terrace, the Spanish engineers reduced the overall length of the exterior walls and built them in the shape of a diamond instead of the standard square pattern[1]. The Presidio of San Vicente was thus relocated from San Saba (near modern Menard) in Texas[23].

On January 1, 1774, O'Conor installed Captain Don Francisco Martinez in command of the Presidio of San Vicente which was still under construction. By April 14, seven barracks were completed and the wall and main bastian work was well underway. Troops at San Vicente patrolled from the east end of Mariscal Canyon southeast to modern Musquiz, while the troops from San Carlos patrolled from San Carlos to the west end of Mariscal Canyon, generally adhering to the boundary of the states of Chihuahua to the west and Coahuila y Tejas to the east[1].

The Apaches, however, continued to raid the defenseless colonists on the northern frontier, and, in 1777, Teodoro de Croix, Commandant General of the Interior Provinces, revised the strategy of O'Conor and advocated a more aggressive policy toward the Apaches. De Croix rearranged the presidial line and closed the presidio at San Vicente in 1781. He created the citizen militia at San Carlos to augment the regular presidio troops in 1782, and although San Vicente was closed, San Carlos was able to outfit about 300 combat-ready troops. Colonel Don Juan de Ugalde, who succeeded Teodoro de Croix, waged an unrelenting campaign against the Apaches in northern frontier and Texas during the decade of the 1780's. The Apaches finally negotiated a peace in March, 1789[1].

The Comanches were yet to come.

67   **San Vicente, Mexico.** Authorized as a military colony in 1850[1], San Vicente, Coahuila was a small farming community of about 200 residents by 1980[3].

A little known fact...

Quien vive?

The password of the revolution.

The revolutionary followers of Pancho Villa, some of whom were most likely just opportunistic bandits, used the community of San Vicente as a base from which to terrorize the communities along both sides of the Rio Grande.

On the night of the Glenn Springs raid, May 5, 1916, Captain Wood and neighbor Oscar de Montel were aroused by the shooting and disturbance at Glenn Springs. When the two arrived at the village to investigate, the bandits shouted "Quien vive? (who lives)[120]."

Montel responded: "Quien es (who is it)?" The answer he received was a flurry of bullets. The bandits were expecting the code: "Viva Villa."

Montel and Woods were forced to take cover until daybreak[80].

La Clocha

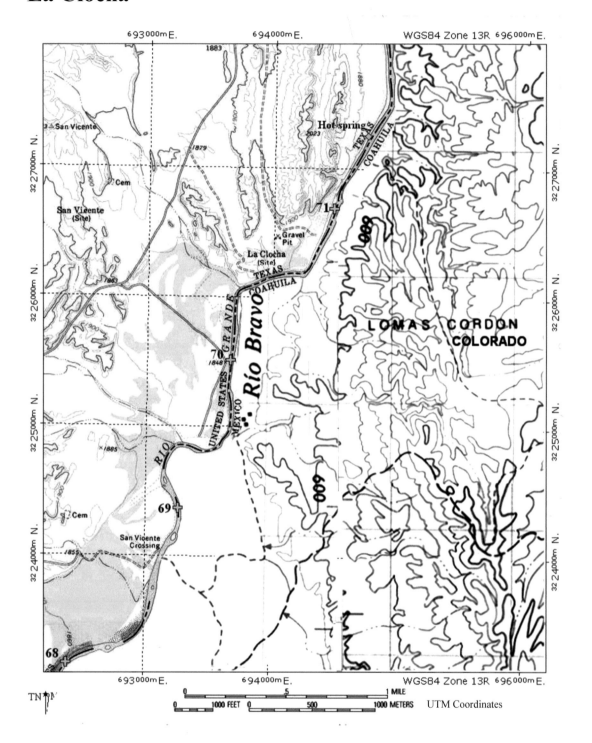

693000m E.   694000m E.   WGS84 Zone 13R 696000m E.

32 27000m N.
32 26000m N.
32 25000m N.
32 24000m N.

San Vicente
Cem
San Vicente
(Site)

Hot springs

TEXAS
COAHUILA

Gravel
Pit
La Clocha
(Site)

TEXAS
COAHUILA

71

70

Río Bravo

RIO GRANDE

UNITED STATES
MEXICO

LOMAS CORDON
COLORADO

Cem
San Vicente
Crossing

69

68

TN

0   5   1 MILE
0   1000 FEET 0   500   1000 METERS   UTM Coordinates

Mile   Description

68   **San Vicente Crossing.** Camping is prohibited in Texas and discouraged in Mexico within 1/2 mile of San Vicente Crossing. A flood in 1966 changed the course of the Rio Grande and the Old San Vicente Crossing Road was abandoned for the new crossing road about a mile upstream[3].

70   **San Vicente, Texas.** About 1896, Mexican immigrants working in the mines at Boquillas del Carmen founded the community of San Vicente, Texas. The village thrived for a half century as a series of small farms in the floodplain of the Rio Grande[1]. The school, where J. O. Langford taught 30 students in 1911 was a single room adobe building, roofed with shingles, with a fireplace at one end and a door at the other, and two glass windows on each side[106]. It provided a place for the education of the local children through 1947 whenever a teacher was available[70].

The importance of the community twice brought the military activity to the site. In March, 1912, twenty-five soldiers from Marathon were stationed in the village for a few months to protect against the threat of Mexican raiders[70]. Later, during World War II, an auxiliary airfield was established at San Vicente.

By 1947, there were only a dozen Mexican families living at San Vicente[59]. When the village was razed by BBNP, the residents scattered to many parts of West Texas[14]. By the early 1970's, nearly all traces of San Vicente, TX had disappeared from maps of the area[59]. Today, only the ruins of a few rock houses, the slab foundation of the school, and the cemetery, with 37 graves[17], are indications of the once vibrant community.

La Clocha Campsite (BBNP). La Clocha is Spanish for "crusher". At one time, a rock crusher was located at this Primitive Backcountry Campsite. Now, it is a popular fishing camp[3].

Gravel Pit Campsite (BBNP). This Primitive Backcountry Campsite was the location of a gravel pit in the early days of the park. Gravel from the site was used for the maintenance of park roads[3].

71   **Hot springs (TX).** A number of hot springs bubble up in the river bed along the west bank of the Rio Grande.

Photo Credit: Louis F. Aulbach

The cemetery at San Vicente, Texas is the most prominent feature remaining of this once prosperous and thriving community on the floodplain near Boquillas. The elegant funerary monuments reveal the importance of this Hispanic village and its people in this region of the Big Bend.

Hot Springs

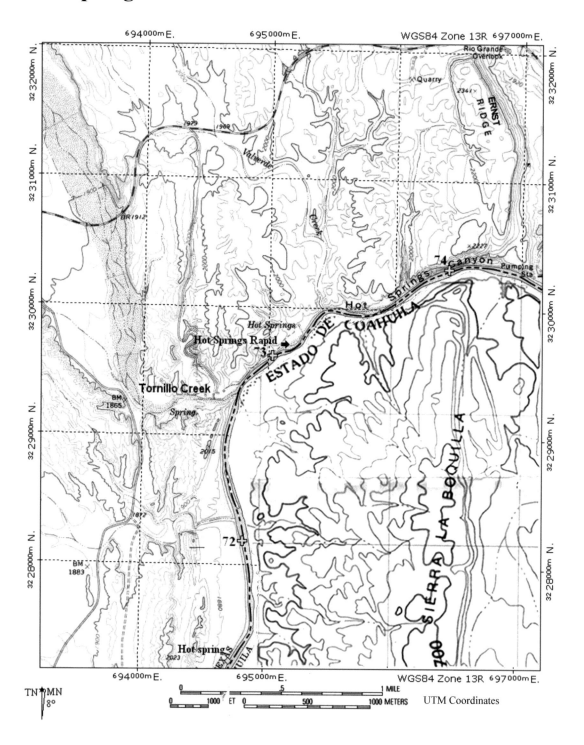

Mile   Description

72   **Tornillo Creek (TX).** Camping is prohibited in Texas and discouraged in Mexico from 1/2 mile upriver of Tornillo Creek to the downstream end of the Boquillas Canyon trail[72].

This drainage was named Pedracitas Creek on the 1855 map of Texas[125], but on the 1884 Military Map of Texas, the creek is named Tornillo Creek[125]. Tornillo means "screw" in Spanish and it is indicative of the screwbean mesquite that grew along its banks[2].

73   **Langford's Hot Springs, Texas.** In 1909, Joseph Oscar Langford homesteaded Section 50, Block G17 which included the land around the hot springs[1]. He then built a small health resort around the bath house he constructed over the 105 degree hot spring[2]. The complex was the first recreational and tourist activity in the Big Bend[8]. Langford operated the Hot Springs until 1942 when he sold the property to the state for inclusion in the national park[2].

Maggy Smith operated the Hot Springs[8] as a concession for the National Park Service until 1952[2] when a half century of commercial activity at the site ended. Nevertheless, the many pictographs and petroglyphs on the rock walls and the mortar holes near Hot Springs attest to the fact that native peoples have used the hot springs for thousands of years[78].

Hot Springs was added to the National Register of Historic Places in 1974[46].

Hot Springs Rapid - Class II

Valverde Creek (TX).

Hot Springs Canyon. This short, and quite beautiful, canyon lets you know that you are nearing Rio Grande Village and the take out, if that is your option, about one mile downstream. The stands of tall tamarisk trees give this canyon a unique feeling.

Photo Credit: Louis F. Aulbach

Photo Credit: Terry Burgess

J. O. Langford built his bath house over the spring with the help of Herman Jacobs, a 25 year old German homesteader on 8 sections near McKinney Hills. Langford wrote his name and the date of construction, 1912, in the concrete of one of the tubs.

People have flocked to the curative waters of the hot springs for centuries. The petroglyphs (above) and pictographs record the thoughts of pre-European users of the springs.

Photo Credit: Linda Gorski

You just never know whom you might meet at the hot springs!

The author was pleased to find that Santa (left) had stopped by for a quick dip before heading off to his next assignment. Phil Flory and his wife Ina Ruth hail from Hillside, Colorado. Flory has been playing Santa for years in Harlingen.

Herman Jacobs had apprenticed as a stone mason in Germany, and the fine quality of his masonry in the construction of the bath house can be seen in the remnants of the foundation and the walls.

Rio Grande Village

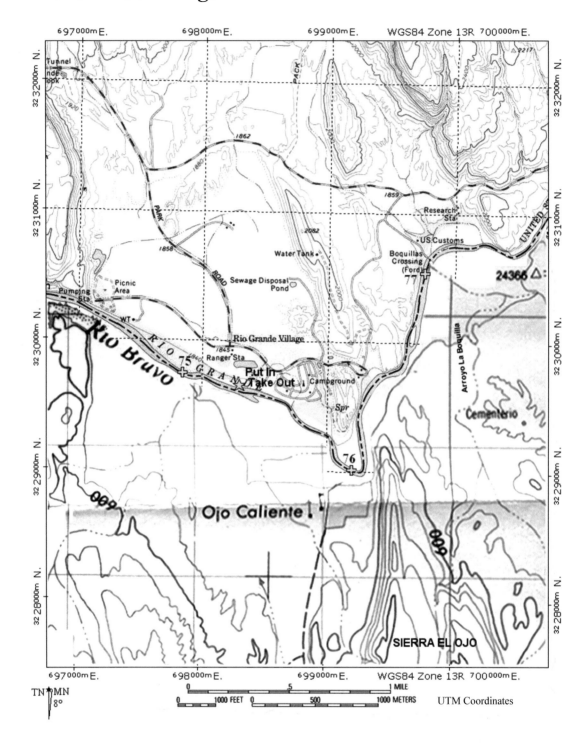

| Mile | Description |

74   **Pumping station (TX).** The nearby Daniels Farm House and Complex was originally built by John Wedin in the early 1920's. Joe Graham purchased the farm in 1926, and it was the headquarters of the cotton farming operation of John R. Daniels from 1937 to 1942[1].

75   **Rio Grande Village (TX). Campground (BBNP). River Access / Put in / Take out** is located opposite the Group Campsite. See more on Rio Grande Village and Boquillas on page 26.

       Ojo Caliente, Mexico. - "hot spring"

77   **Boquillas Crossing.** In May, 2002, the unofficial border crossing historically used at Boquillas was closed by the Border Patrol[128].

       Arroyo La Boquilla (Mex) - "the mouth-piece"

       US Customs / Research Station. Site of Ed Lindsey's home and store, 1894 - 1900.

Photo Credit: Louis F. Aulbach

The innovative stock watering facility on the Ojo Caliente flood-plain uses natural materials to provide access to the river for livestock while preventing the animals from wandering into Rio Grande Village.

A little known fact...

The high peak of the Sierra del Carmen which rises above the entrance to Boquillas Canyon is known as Schott Tower[37].

In November, 1852, the survey party under Marine Tyler Wickham Chandler and 2Lt. Duff C. Green noted the crumbling presidio at San Vicente. They continued across the terrain to the mouth of another canyon which Chandler named Canon de Sierra Carmel (now, Boquillas Canyon) where they camped and waited to be re-supplied. While camped at the mouth of Bo-quillas Canyon, the survey party decided to abandon the further survey of the Rio Grande because of the difficult nature of the terrain that lay ahead[1].

With this survey party was Arthur C. V. Schott, a naturalist, engineer and physician. Schott signed on as a draftsman with the bound-ary survey team of 1852 and his sketches of the scenes of the Rio Grande are among the earliest known visual records of Big Bend. The peak above the Boquillas entrance is named for him[120].

Since the peak is in Mexico, it does not appear on the USGS 7.5 Minute Topo map which omits the topography south of the Rio Grande. Geographic naming conventions, which may be in common usage in the United States, are frequently not used on the Mexican topographic maps. As a result, the designation of Schott Tower has fallen into disuse in recent years.

Photo Credit: Fraser Baker

The Rio Grande Village River Access is located near the Group Campsite. It provides easy access to the river for loading and unloading gear and boats.

Boquillas Canyon

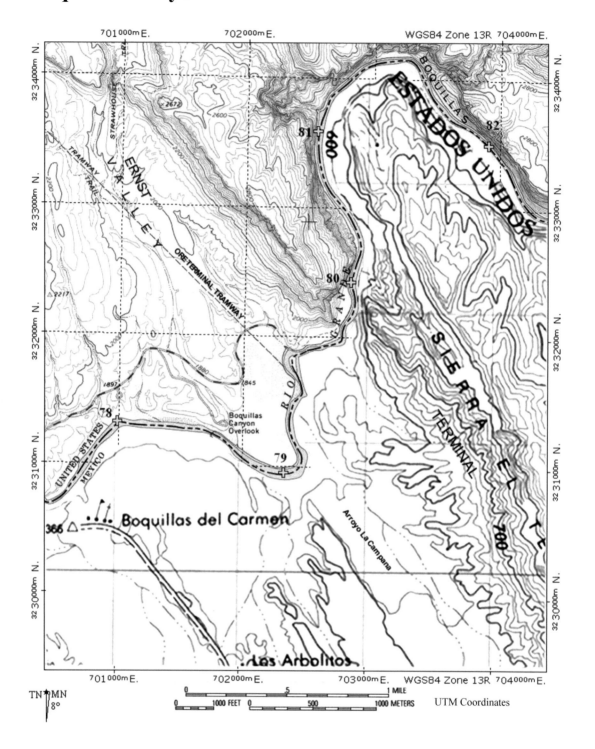

TN MN
8°

UTM Coordinates

Mile	Description

77 **Boquillas del Carmen, Mexico.** See page 25.

78 **Boquillas Canyon Overlook (TX).**

79 **Arroyo La Campana (Mex)** - "the bell"

Ore Terminal Aerial Tramway.

80 **Boquillas Canyon.**

Sierra el Terminal (Mex). The Mexican ore terminal was located on the lower slopes of this mountain, about a mile from the river.

Remnants of the Aerial Tramway that carried ore from the mines in Mexico to the terminal in Ernst Valley lie generally undisturbed across the desert where the tram system operated early in the 20th century. Ore buckets (top), wire cable and wooden towers, in various states of disrepair, can be seen along the original route of the tramway. The plaque (left) on the bucket identifies the A. Leschen & Sons Rope Company of St. Louis as the manufacturer of the tramway system.

The village of Boquillas, Mexico sits atop a rocky outcrop above the Rio Grande. The heights of the Sierra Del Carmen rise above the town in the background. In 1902, Boquillas del Carmen was destroyed by a flood and it was relocated in 1903 to its present site on higher ground.

Puerto Rico

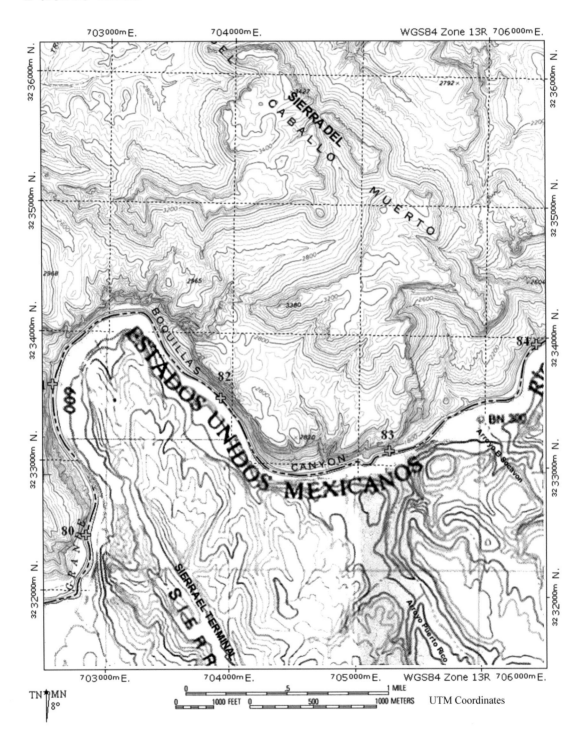

Mile   Description

83   Arroyo Puerto Rico (Mex).

Arroyo El Socavon (Mex) - "the cavern"

Sierra del Caballo Muerto (TX) - "Dead Horse Mountains" - The Sierra del Caballo Muerto is the subrange of the Sierra Del Carmen which extends into Texas. Black bear were known to live in the Sierra del Caballo Muerto until the 1930's[137], and local ranchers have made sightings as recently as 2005. The only recorded sighting of a coati in the Trans Pecos was made in these mountains in 1939[137].

The name seems to evoke the special mystery and the Spanish influence in this harsh and wild frontier, but the true origin of the name is not known. There are, in fact, several stories of the origin of the name:
(1) The name may date to Spanish explorers or soldiers traveling in the area during the 1700's and attempting to subdue the hostile Apaches[137].
(2) The name stems from an episode in 1881 when Texas Rangers under Capt. Charles Nevill captured some Indian ponies in a canyon in the mountains and slaughtered them so the Indians could not recover them[137].
(3) The name derives from the tale of two cowboys in the 1880's who found a remuda of horses trapped in a canyon and were unable to rescue them as they watched them starve to death[137].
(4) Government surveyor Arthur A. Stiles, conducting "naming meetings" in 1903 for regional place names coined the Caballo Muerto name for a favorite saddle horse of his that fell to its death in the mountains[137].
(5) J. O. Langford, who settled in the area in 1909, retold the story that the mountains in Texas got their name from Dead Horse Canyon where Brewster County ranchers who were smuggling a herd of horses from Mexico corralled them in the small box canyon. When they learned that the Texas Rangers were in pursuit, the ranchers abandoned the horses to starve to death. His story seems to have combined elements of the two other stories[106].

A review of the historical maps of the area are of little help. Although several of the early maps are very general, the current name does not appear on maps up to 1923. The 1855 Map of Texas shows the range of mountains as the Horse Head Mountains. Similarly, Pressler's Map of Texas in 1858 identifies them as Horse-Head Hills. The 1882 Map of Texas shows the whole range of mountains as the Sierra de Santiago. The Santiago name persists on the 1914 Official Railway and County Map of Texas and on the 1923 Rand McNally Map[125].

One cannot help but think, however, that the early association of the mountains with "horses" gives some credence to an origin in the earliest Spanish times.

The sandbar in the first bend of the river within the confines of Boquillas Canyon is frequently used as the first night's camp for trips through the canyon. Located in Mile 81, this camp can be reached on the short day of paddling from the Rio Grande Village put in that follows the long shuttle for this section.

Photo Credit: Fraser Baker

Chupadero

Mile   Description

84   Arroyo El Chupadero (Mex).

       Wax factory site (Mex).

       Arroyo La Fragua (Mex) - "the forge"

86   Creek (Mex).

Photo Credit: Fraser Baker

A close up of Lizard Rock.

Photo Credit: Louis F. Aulbach

The reflective symmetry showcases the extraordinary beauty of Boquillas Canyon near Chupadero Canyon where the Lizard Rock is crawling up the side of the canyon wall.

Marufo Vega

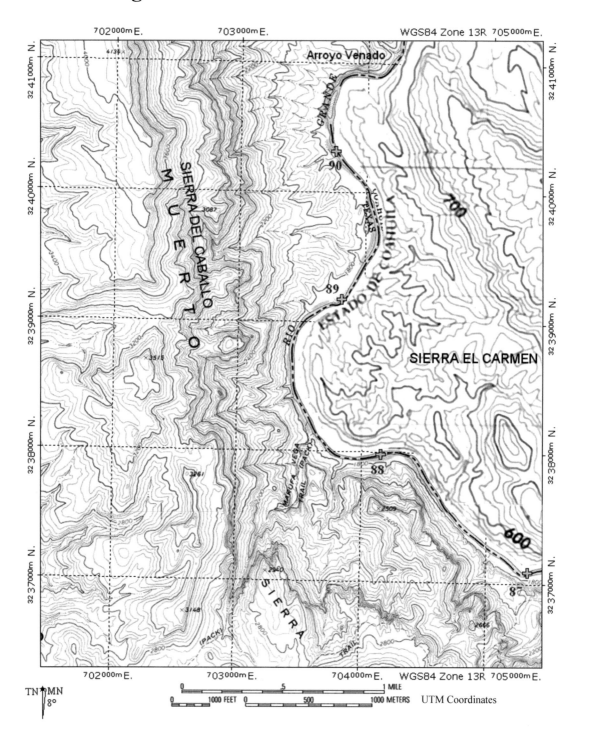

Mile   Description

88   **Marufo Vega Trail (TX).** The six mile hiking trail to the river starts on the road near the Boquillas Canyon Overlook and follows the Ore Terminal Trail through a drainage past two wooden towers before heading east at the Strawhouse Trail Junction[4]. Later, it forks into two routes descending to the Rio Grande. The trail was commonly used by Mexicans traveling from Boquillas and San Vicente to the Adams Ranch[4], a major wax processing center in the area, and it is named, using a slightly variant spelling, for the prominent resident of San Vicente, Texas, Gregorio Marufo[14].

Gregorio Marufo was born in Mexico in May, 1856, and married Natividad Ferro in 1883[14]. They immigrated to Texas in 1891, and in 1900, Marufo was working as a laborer in Marathon where he lived with his wife Natividad, age 36, sons Jesus, age 17, also a laborer, Marianno, age 3, and Anecito, age 1, and infant daughter Lina[109].

The Marufo family moved to San Vicente, Texas after the turn of the century and by 1903, he was a successful floodplain farmer growing wheat and vegetables. News reports in the Alpine Avalanche on May 1, 1903 celebrated his farming skills as he harvested a 260 pound pumpkin among his crops[14].

During the first decades of the twentieth century, Marufo was a man of importance in the San Vicente, Texas, village. He lived in a fine, two room rock house and owned a big farm with numerous goats, chickens and pigs[106]. He also served on the school board at La Noria[14]. But, by 1920, Gregorio Marufo was living in retirement with his son in law Guadalupe Gaston, residing on land adjacent to his old friend Clemente Mena[52].

90   **Arroyo Venado (TX)** - "the deer"

        Arroyo Venado Rapid. Class I-III.

Photo Credit: Louis F. Aulbach

The flat top butte signals your approach to Arroyo La Fragua in Mile 84 (right).

Sometime prior to February, 2014, a rock fall from the cliff on the Mexican side near Arroyo Venado added several huge boulders to the river. The Venado Rapid now has several large rocks to negotiate. Below is the view looking upstream to the new boulders in the rapid. The flow in the picture below is about 400 cfs. At higher levels, the rapid can become a Class III rapid.

Photo Credit: Louis F. Aulbach

Rabbit Ears

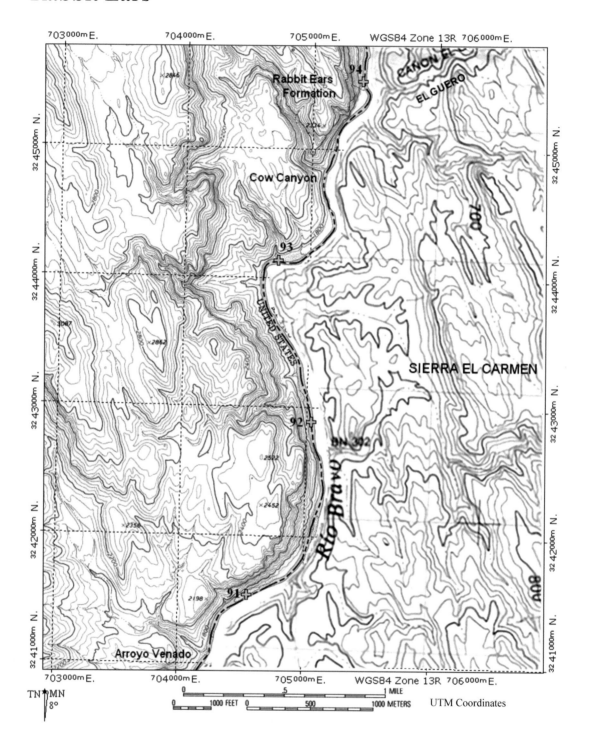

Mile   Description

90   **Arroyo Venado (TX)** - "the deer"

        Arroyo Venado Rapid. Class I. The rapid here is frequently non-existent.

91   **Arroyo "BN302" (Mex).** A large, grassy sandbar at the mouth of this canyon makes a good campsite.

92   **Creek (Mex).**

93   **Cow Canyon (TX).** - "la vaca"

        Canon El Guero (Mex). The outwash from this canyon creates a large, grassy sandbar which is a popular campsite. The canyon offers interesting hikes into the mountains, however, the access to the canyon requires some climbing since there is a steep pour off a short distance into the canyon that must be negotiated. A good rope can help.

        Rabbit Ears Formation (TX) - "oídos del conejo"

Rabbit Ears (right) is immediately upstream of Canon El Guero (below), but on the Texas side of the river. The major obstacle to Canon El Guero is beyond this suspended boulder.

Heath Creek

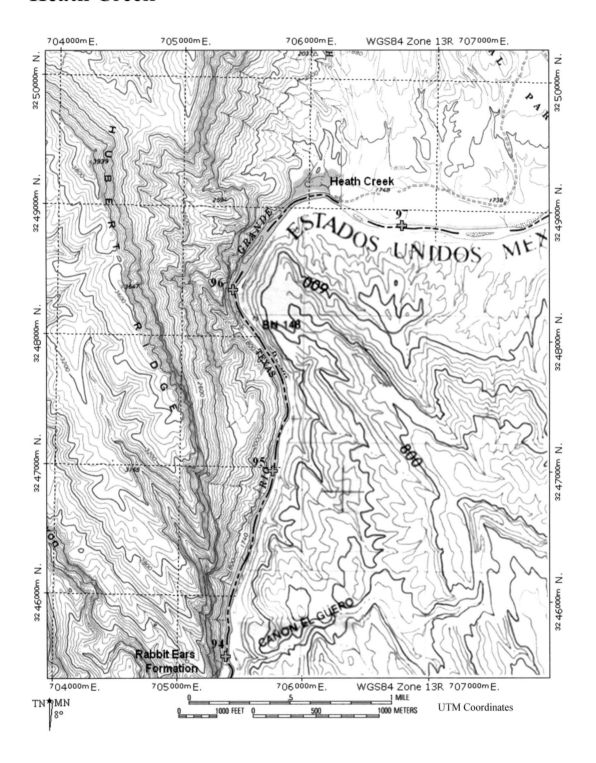

UTM Coordinates

Mile   Description

96   Heath Creek (TX).

A little known fact...

On a recent trip through Boquillas Canyon in February, 2006, we came across two candelilla wax camps on the Mexican side of the river. Both camps were inactive, but each site showed signs that it was only temporarily dormant and would revive when the time for harvesting the candelilla plant is right.

Candelilla wax, although not well known to the general public, is a primary ingredient in many products in common use across America, including floor wax, cosmetics, such as lipstick, candles and chewing gum, such as the popular Chiclets brand[49]. Check the ingredients label on your next purchase.

For many years, candelilla wax was used by residents of the desert to make candles, religious statues and artificial flowers. The wax was also used in waterproofing leather, cloth and matches. Mass production of candelilla wax began in the first decade of the twentieth century. Texan Ralph Ogden, who claimed to have learned about the wax from a padre at a Spanish mission who made candles, was the first to attempt the commercial production of candelilla wax when he established a wax factory in Mexico around 1910[49]. Over the next four decades, other large scale operations were built at Glenn Springs, at the middle Tornillo Creek community, at the Asa Jones site in the Lower Canyons and at the Adams Ranch. However, since the 1930's, the production of candelilla wax has primarily been concentrated in transient camps along the Rio Grande. The wax camps persist, even today, because the extraction of candelilla wax has

The steel vat, or caldera, with hinged grates, lies ready for use.

been one of the most profitable economic activities in the Chihuahuan Desert for the last 100 years[49].

Wax camps tend to be located in remote side canyons where candelilla is plentiful so the camp can operate for several months. A typical camp consists of a vat, or calera, a firepit, stock piles of candelilla, piles of the cooked plant, called yerba seca, sleeping shelters, sun shades and brush fences. Candelilleros, as the wax makers are called, take only a few items into camp, such as the vat, burros and packsaddles, machetes, burlap bags, rope, jars of acid, cooking pots, staple food and a change of clothes. They are adept at living off the land[49].

The vat, usually 6 ft long, 3 ft wide and 3 ft deep, is fabricated from sheet steel with heavy steel grates hinged on the ends. Hauled in by donkeys, the vat is set up near the river on the first terrace and it can be used repeatedly for many years. Many tools are fabricated by the candelilleros. A wax skimmer is made from a flattened and perforated tin can. Pitchforks are fashioned from mesquite trees. A tortilla griddle comes from the end of a steel drum. Twine and rope are made from sotol and lechuguilla. Rock shelters, small cavities and crevices in the limestone walls of the side canyons serve as individual living units for the candelilleros and provide shelter and storage for tools and possessions[49].

Working in small groups, the candelilleros can gather plants and extract about 1,000 pounds of candelilla wax per month. During the late 1970's, David Adams of the Adams Ranch at Stillwell Crossing, one of two major candelilla wax dealers in Texas, was marketing as much as 60,000 pounds of refined wax per month at $1.50 per pound[49].

John Rich rests in a typical shelter and tool shed for a candelillero. Shovels and other tools are stored on a shelf behind him, while there is a flat living space and kitchen area to the side.

El Indio

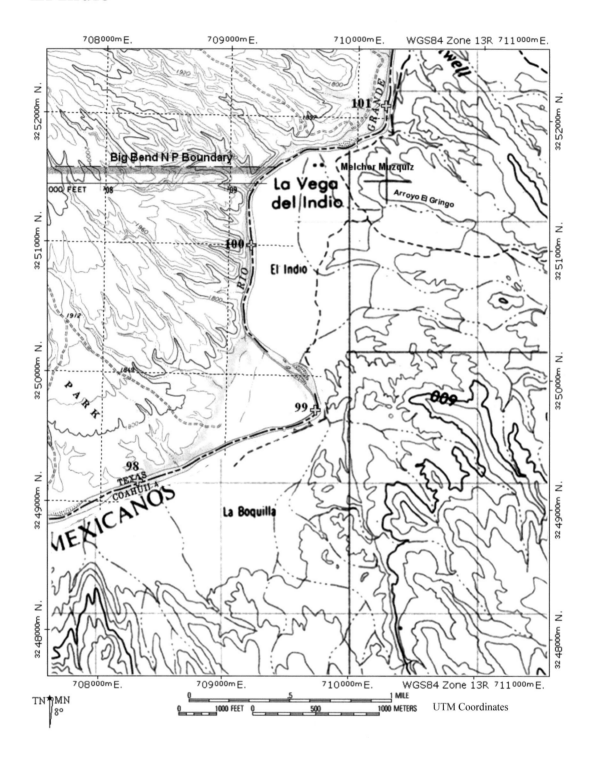

TN MN
8°

UTM Coordinates

Mile	Description

97 **Creek (Mex).**

98 **Creek (Mex).**

La Boquilla, Mexico.

99 **El Indio, Mexico.**

100 **Big Bend National Park Boundary (TX).**

Creek (Mex).

La Vega del Indio (Mex).

Melchor Muzquiz, Mexico.

Arroyo El Gringo (Mex). - "the gringo"

A little known fact...

Have you ever wondered where the Telephone Canyon Trail goes?

Telephone Canyon and its little used trail wind through the Sierra del Caballo Muerto[3] to the ruins of a military encampment on the extreme eastern edge of Big Bend National Park.

As a response to the border unrest during the Villa Revolution, the Fourth Texas Infantry of the National Guard established Camp Mercer in 1916 on a gravel terrace overlooking the floodplain of the Rio Grande a little over two miles upstream of Stillwell Crossing. Communication with the main camp at La Noria was made over telephone lines laid through the canyon that bears that name[139].

Only the ruins of a few rock houses and a large rock corral remain of this isolated outpost.

Photo Credit: Louis F. Aulbach

The long straight away, with La Boquilla floodplain on river right, looks directly toward two notable peaks in the distance. On the left is Cerro La Hormiga (the ant), and on the right is Cerro La Salada whose northeast flank is the site of La Seis fluorite mine, now abandoned, one of many in the area.

Stillwell

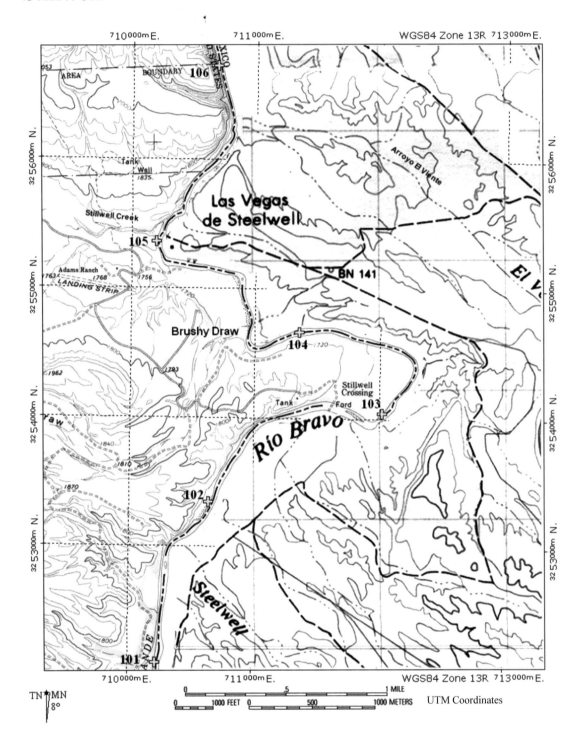

Mile   Description

101   **Arroyo Steelwell (Mex).**

102   **Creek (Mex).**

          Creek (Mex).

          Creek (Mex).

          Stillwell Crossing.

104   **Brushy Draw (TX).**

          Adams Ranch, Texas.

105   **Stillwell Creek (TX).**

          Las Vegas de Steelwell (Mex).

          Black Gap Wildlife Management Area Boundary (TX).

          Creek (Mex).

This old water tank on the Adams Ranch reminds us of the extensive candelilla wax operations on the ranch.

John Rich sets up his tent on the island campsite near Stillwell Crossing. Campsites are scarce in this section of the river, and camping is prohibited on private property in the vicinity of the Adams Ranch headquarters without prior approval.

La Linda

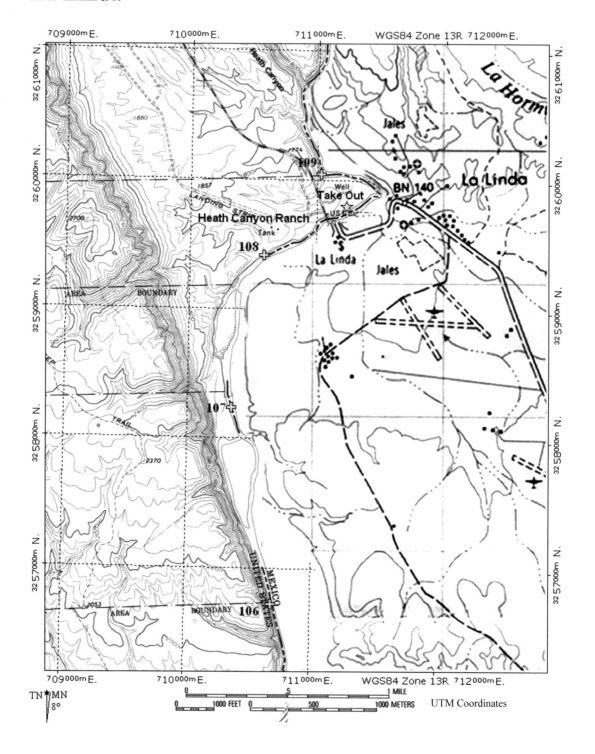

Mile   Description

106   **Black Gap Wildlife Management Area Boundary (TX).**

         Black Gap Rapid. Class II-III. This rapid is the most difficult on the Boquillas Canyon section. At low water levels, the large rocks in mid stream create obstacles that are difficult to avoid. The rapid is easily lined.

107   **Black Gap Wildlife Management Area Boundary (TX).**

108   **Heath Canyon Ranch,** Texas. Former housing facilities for the DuPont Corporation, purchased and renovated by Andy Kurie as a tourist resort.

         La Linda, Mexico. See page 31.

         Gerstacker Bridge. Built in 1968 and
         named for Carl A. Gerstacker; renamed the Hallie Stillwell Memorial Bridge. Closed in 1997.

Photo Credit: Louis F. Aulbach

Take Out (TX). Site of the cattle ford pioneered by rancher Tom Heath around 1900.

Arroyo El Viente (Mex) - "number 20"

John Rich lines Black Gap Rapid (right).

Photo Credit: Louis F. Aulbach

After passing under the Gerstacker Bridge, the take out is on the gravel bar on river left near the site of the low water crossing. The fluorspar plant sits on the bluff above the river which makes a sharp left turn.

Permits and Regulations

When the river level exceeds 3,000 cubic feet per second (cfs) on the gauge at Johnson's Ranch, permits will be limited on river sections of class III or greater difficulty (Santa Elena Canyon, Mariscal Canyon, and Lower Canyons) to inflatable rafts with a minimum of three air compartments (excluding thwarts) and minimum dimensions of 12'x6'; decked canoes and kayaks capable of excluding water when used with a spray skirt; open canoes at least 50% filled with floatation; dories; and sport yaks. The restriction does not apply to parties that portage rapids of Class III or greater difficulty in Mariscal Canyon or the Lower Canyons; be aware, however, that portaging is not always possible.

All human waste must be carried out for river trips between the Santa Elena Take-out and La Linda. Kayak-only or single canoe trips, however, are exempt from this requirement. Portable toilets are available for rent from several river trip outfitters.

The Superintendent of Big Bend National Park may close to public use portions of the Rio Grande when necessary for public safety or for resource protection.

Equipment Checklist

Required Equipment

A Park Ranger may inspect your boat for required equipment while you are on the river. The following equipment is essential for a safe river trip:

• Boat: Canoes, kayaks, or heavy duty inflatable rafts.
• Dump-station compatible carry-out toilet: To pack out human waste.
• Life jackets: One U.S. Coast Guard approved life jacket per person. Must be worn on class II or greater water (International Scale). Must be worn on inner tubes or air mattresses. Bring one extra per group.
• Paddles/Oars: Each vessel (except inner tubes and air mattresses) must carry an extra paddle or oar, except for kayaks, which must carry one extra paddle per party.
• Patch kit/pump: All inflatable vessels, except inner tubes and air mattresses, must carry a patch kit and pump.

Recommended Items

The following gear is recommended to increase safety, reduce impacts to the environment, and make your trip more enjoyable:

• First aid kit: To handle major and minor emergencies.
• Plastic trash bags: Carry out all trash.
• Safety line: Rope length 50'-100' and 3/8" diameter. Carry tie-downs to secure gear in your vessel.
• Bailing bucket: To remove water from inside your vessel.
• Water-tight containers: To keep food, clothing, gear dry.
• Small shovel
• Flashlight.

For a Safe and Legal Trip:

• Get a permit.
• Report all injuries or property damage or losses over $100 to a Park Ranger.
• Treat any water collected for drinking.
• Carry out all litter including cigarette butts and toilet paper.
• Carry out human waste. Dump stations are located at Santa Elena Canyon, the Chisos Basin, Rio Grande Village, and at Stillwell Store and RV Park on FM2627.
• Urinate in the river or on wet shoreline.
• Use a fire pan if you build a campfire. A stove is better to protect the environment.
• Burn only charcoal or dead and down wood from the floodplain in a fire pan.
• Carry out all floatable debris. The common method is to place fire remains in a bucket of water, remove floating material to garbage sack, and pour remainder in main river current.
• Wear a USCG approved life jacket. A type I, III, or V personal flotation device is required for Santa Elena, Mariscal, and the Lower Canyons.
• Carry gear in waterproof bags and boxes, leashed in to prevent loss in event of an upset.
• Scout all major rapids and consider portaging.
• Camp well above the high water mark and out of any side canyons.
• Respect private property in both countries.
• Have a fun, but safe trip!

DO NOT:

• Operate any vessel in a reckless or negligent manner.
• Overload vessels.
• Use firearms or explosives. They are prohibited.
• Disturb natural, historic or prehistoric features along the river.
• Forget to secure boats with lines at night as sudden river rises do occur.
• Take your pet on the river.
• Jug-fish in Big Bend National Park.
• Collect or disturb rocks, plants, wildlife, or any historical or archeological objects in the park and along the Rio Grande Wild and Scenic River.

• Float on inner tubes in Santa Elena Canyon, Mariscal Canyon, and the Lower Canyons.

Swimming in the Rio Grande is not recommended. The river can be hazardous, even in calm-looking water. Be aware of strong undercurrents, shallow areas with sharp rocks and large tree limbs, and be watchful for trot lines with large hooks.

River Use Regulations for Big Bend National Park and the Rio Grande Wild and Scenic River

For the river environment's protection and your safety, observe these regulations on both sides of the river and on private land along the Rio Grande Wild and Scenic River.

Any river user must obtain a National Park Service permit (a $10 fee) before watercraft is placed or operated on the Rio Grande within Big Bend National Park and for overnight trips on the Rio Grande Wild and Scenic River downstream from the park. Day-use inner tubes are exempt. You are required to complete a customs declaration form if you camp on the Mexican side of the river.

Each person will have a U.S. Coast Guard-approved personal flotation device (PFD), which is properly fitted, in serviceable condition, and immediately accessible. Day-use inner tubers are exempt. Type I, III or V PFDs are required for Santa Elena, Mariscal, and the Lower Canyons. PFDs must be worn in Class II or greater difficulty whitewater.

Each vessel shall carry an extra paddle or oar; kayaks shall have an extra paddle per party. Paddles are not required for air mattresses or inner tubes.

Each group using inflatable vessels will carry an operable pump and a patch kit capable of making major repairs.

No vessel shall carry more than a safe load, in persons or total weight, considering type of craft, intended use area, and water and weather conditions.

Inner tubes are not allowed in the Lower Canyons.

Starts and Group Size

On the Rio Grande Wild and Scenic River downstream from Big Bend National Park, the group size limit is 20 people for private groups. Commercial operators may start a maximum of 20 persons per day, not including guides.

No more than three parties per day may be started by any group, organization, or commercial operator. River parties must start at least 2 hours apart.

Individual river groups must travel, camp, and eat lunch separate from other groups.

Respect property rights and do not trespass on posted land.

Firearms, other weapons, explosives, and traps are prohibited.

Pets are not permitted on the river or in any other part of the backcountry.

The destruction, injury, defacement, removal, or disturbance of any natural or cultural feature is prohibited.

The Rio Grande canyons contain critical peregrine falcon habitat.

River users must contain campfires in firepans. Burn only charcoal or down and dead wood. Carry out all floatable remnants of the fire; non-floatable debris should be carried out, or may be disposed of in the main current of the river. Reduce impacts by using only charcoal or self-contained stoves.

Deposit refuse, including cigarette butts and toilet paper, only in facilities designed for that purpose at take-outs or subsequent points. Strain liquids, including dishwater, and deposit them in the river. Carry out strained materials.

All solid human waste must be carried out, with the following exception: kayak-only or single-canoe trips.

Report any accident with an injury or property damage of $100 or more to the NPS.

Recommendations

The NPS recommends the following for your safety and the protection of the river environment:

Wear PFDs at all times; carry one extra per trip. Type II PFDs (horse collar) are not allowed in Santa Elena, Mariscal, or the Lower Canyons and not recommended in the other sections.

Each river party should carry a suitable amount of survival gear, including a first aid kit, extra water, sun protection, rain gear, a throw line, and an extra rope at least 50 feet long and 3/8 inch in diameter.

The safe capacity for inflatable craft should be considered 1/2 the manufacturer's rated load. If no such rating can be found, the mid-line of the boat should be at least 2 inches above the water line. The safe capacity for canoes is no more than 2 persons and 100 pounds of gear in Class III or greater whitewater.

All major rapids should be scouted. Consider portaging.

Springs may be contaminated. Treat water from a natural source before drinking.

Because sudden river rises occur, camp well above the high water mark and out of any side canyon or arroyo. Secure boats with ropes and tie each craft separately.

In the event of an emergency, an "X" marked on the ground by any means visible from the air signifies that help is needed. Carry two 3-by-10-foot strips of international orange colored material and a signal mirror. Flights over the river are limited, so do not count on being spotted quickly.

Water Quality in the Rio Grande
Information for River Rafters

The quality of water in the Rio Grande through the Big Bend region is highly variable. Big Bend National Park staff samples the water for bacterial levels on a monthly basis at several locations within the park. The samples require 24 hours for incubation, delaying results and preventing timely notification of poor water quality conditions. However, the sample results have shown some trends between river flow levels and high bacteria counts.

The data shows that just after rainstorms and when flow levels are rising the bacterial counts rise and may exceed the recommended levels for contact recreation such as swimming. This is likely caused by runoff from creeks and other tributaries carrying animal waste and other pollutants into the Rio Grande. This occurs primarily during the summer monsoon season, between June and October, but can happen at any time of year.

Bacteria, such as Fecal Coliform and E. Coli, can cause illness if ingested. Children are particularly susceptible to bacterial infection. Small children are more likely to be exposed through splashing, and otherwise getting river water in their eyes, mouths, ears or nose.

On the other hand, during periods of prolonged low flows, the bacterial levels tend to be very low, and well within safe limits of state standards for recreation. During low flows, the river tends to be high in salts as is common in desert rivers below dams. The high salinity may reduce the amount of bacteria in the water during low flows. Because many of the small communities along the river do not have adequate sewage treatment facilities, there may be bacteria in the water immediately downstream of these towns even during periods of low flow.

People who raft and canoe down the river will probably not be at high risk, however precautions should be taken to reduce the chances of ingesting river water, especially by children.

What precautions should you take on the river?
 * Never drink river water
 * Boil river water for 10 minutes prior to use for rinsing dishes, etc.
 * Disinfect cuts or other open sores after exposure to river water
 * Prevent children from immersing their heads in the water or otherwise getting water into their mouth, eyes, ears or nose.

During and soon after high flows and/or rainstorms:
 * Avoid prolonged exposure to the river water (i.e. don't spend long periods of time swimming)
 * Avoid immersing your head in the water.
 * Keep very young children out of the water

Source: Big Bend National Park website.

A little known fact...

In May, 2003, Raymond Skiles, a biologist at Big Bend National Park, reported that the Rio Grande had stopped flowing through Mariscal Canyon[162]. The river did, however, get a recharge a few weeks later.

Although there is some cause for alarm at the lack of flow in the Rio Grande, the conditions are not unique. Similar conditions occurred on several days in the drought years of 1953, 1955, 1957, and 1958 when the gauge at Johnson's Ranch measured zero.

These flow conditions may be somewhat cyclical since the river recovered in subsequent years. The highest daily flow recorded at Johnson's Ranch was recorded on October 1, 1978 when the gauge measured the river running at 65,332 cfs.

There may be hope!

The low water conditions in the Great Unknown can require boaters to walk their boats through the shallow riffles. On this trip in October, 2011, the flow measured at Castolon was 60 cfs and falling.

Photo Credit: Louis F. Aulbach

Footnotes and Bibliographic References

1. Gomez, Arthur R. A Most Singular Country: a history of occupation in the Big Bend. Salt Lake City: Brigham Young University, 1990. Pgs. 24, 25, 27, 28, 29, 31, 33, 34, 36, 39, 41, 59, 61, 64, 68, 72, 75, 77, 89, 90, 93, 100, 101, 103, 107, 109, 110, 113, 114, 115, 116, 117, 119, 121, 122, 125, 126, 127, 129, 131, 133, 134, 139, 141, 142, 148, 149, 156, 157, 158, 159, 160, 161, 162, 163, 165, 166, 167, 168, 171, 172, 173, 174, 176, 190, 202, 203, 211, 213, 214, 218.

2. Pearson, John, editor. Road guide to paved and improved dirt roads of Big Bend National Park. Big Bend National Park: Big Bend Natural History Association, 1980. Pgs. 4, 6, 7, 8, 9, 10, 30, 31, 32, 34, 35, 36, 44.

3. Pearson, John, editor. Road guide to backcountry dirt roads of Big Bend National Park. Big Bend National Park: Big Bend Natural History Association, 1980. Pgs. 3, 6, 7, 12, 13, 14, 15, 16, 18, 19, 20, 22, 23, 25, 26, 27, 28, 29, 32, 33.

4. Pearson, John, editor. Hiker's guide to trails of Big Bend National Park. Big Bend National Park: Big Bend Natural History Assn., 1978. Pgs. 3, 24, 27.

5. "Castolon." Clifford B. Casey Collection, Box 2, Folder 241, Archives of the Big Bend, Sul Ross State University, Alpine, TX.

6. Smithers, W. D. "Residents on the Rio Grande, 1916-1930." Clifford B. Casey Collection, Box 32, Folder 2022e, Archives of the Big Bend, Sul Ross State University, Alpine, TX.

7. "Big Bend National Park Base Map." Clifford B. Casey Collection, Archives of the Big Bend, Sul Ross State University, Alpine, TX.

8. "Historic American Buildings Survey Inventory, Big Bend National Park, 1964." Clifford B. Casey Collection, Archives of the Big Bend, Sul Ross State University, Alpine, TX.

14. Hitchcock, Totsy Nellie. Representative individuals and families of the Lower Big Bend Region, 1895-1925. Masters Thesis. Sul Ross State College. Alpine, Texas. 1960.

16. Willeford, Glenn P. A History of Johnson's Ranch and Trading Post on the Rio Grande, 1927-1943. M. S. Thesis. Sul Ross University, 1993. Pgs. 5, 45, 80, 100.

17. Willeford, Glenn P. and Gerald G. Raun. "Big Bend National Park. An unofficial guide to the cemeteries and gravesites." Ojinaga, Chihuahua, Mexico. <http://ojinaga.com/gravesites/> [Accessed Feb 6 09:02:00 US/Central 2006].

18. Willeford, Glenn P. "Mexican settlers in the Big Bend region of Texas, 1880-1945." Ojinaga, Chihuahua, Mexico. <http://ojinaga.com/MexstlrsBB.html> [Accessed Aug 20 08:02:00 US/Central 2002].

19. Smithers, W. D. "El Pista de Santa Helena [map, 1930?]" Clifford B. Casey Collection, Box 32, Folder 2022e, Archives of the Big Bend, Sul Ross State University, Alpine, TX.

20. Sanchez, Gus. "The original settlers of the Big Bend." The Brown Quarterly, Volume 2, No. 1 (Fall 1997). <http://brownvboard.org/brwnqurt/02-1/02-1d.htm> [Accessed Mar 1 07:34:00 US/Central 2006].

21. Molinar, Monica. "Descendants of Cipriano Hernandez." Alaskan Place. <http://www.alaskanplace.com/spreadingbranches/hernandez.htm> [Accessed Nov 10 18:19:00 US/Central 2002].

23. "Los presidios de Coahuila." Geocities. <http://mx.geocities.com/presidial/lospresidios.htm> [Accessed October 5, 2002].

25. Chapman, Art. "Black Seminole Indians." Virtual Texan. <http://www.virtualtexan.com/writers/chapman/seminole.htm> [Accessed Mar 20 16:32:00 US/Central 2000].

27. Scott, Colonel Darryl A. "Keynote Address. Black Seminole Indian Scout Cemetery Association. September 19, 1998." LWF Communications. <http://www.coax.net/people/lwf/sp_scott.htm> [Accessed Mar 20 16:39:00 US/Central 2000].

28. Williams, Mary L. "Seminole-Negro Indian Scouts." LWF Communications. <http://www.coax.net/people/lwf/scouts.htm> [Accessed Mar 20 16:40:00 US/Central 2000].

29. Bilello, Joseph, et al. "Dorgan-Sublett." Texas Tech University. <http://www.ttu.edu/~arc/hist-pres/dorgan-sublett.htm> [Accessed Nov 15 15:23:00 US/Central 2001].

30. Munn, Wayne A. "A family journey to Big Bend National Park." The Picture Professional Online. Issue 3, 2000. <http://www.aspp.com/latent_images/00_03.htm> [Accessed Nov 13 13:20:00 US/Central 2001].

32. "Alice Taylor Babb." IP Services. <http://www.ip-services.com/shipman/Shipman/Shipman/Esther/> [Accessed October 29, 2002].

33. "Border Healing Woman, Jewel Babb." Geocities. <http://www.geocities.com/shirlrun/jewell.html> [Accessed October 29, 2002].

34. "William (Bill) Babb - Sarah Elizabeth Shipman." Geocities. <http://www.geocities.com/Heartland/Flats/5643/bill.html> [Accessed Oct 29 11:26:00 US/Central 2002].

35. "William Isaac 'Ike' Babb." Geocities. <http://www.geocities.com/Heartland/Flats/5643/ike2.html> [Accessed October 29, 2002].

37. Burleson, Bob. "Suggested river trips through the Rio Grande river canyons in the Big Bend region of Texas, as charted by the Texas Explorers Club." [no date].

39. Administrative History. Big Bend National Park. National Park Service. <http://www.nps.gov/bibe/adhi/adhi1a.htm> [Accessed Apr 1 10:15:00 US/Central 2006]. Ch. 1, 10, 11, 13.

40. Wheat, Jim. "Postmasters and post offices of Brewster County, Texas, 1880-1930." Rootsweb.com <http://www.rootsweb.com/~txpost/brewster.html> [Accessed Apr 1 16:03:00 US/Central 2006].

44. Greenberg, Joel. "A brief history of the Old Ore Terminal." Joel Greenberg. <http://oreterminal.joelandkaren.com/history/history.html> [Accessed Nov 13 08:19:00 US/Central 2005].

45. Brady, Marilyn Dell. "Black Seminole Army Scouts in the Texas Big Bend." Institute of Texan Cultures. <http://www.texascultures.utsa.edu/hiddenhistory/Pages1/brady.htm> [Accessed Mar 9 15:01:00 US/Central 2006].

46. "Texas - Brewster County." National Register of Historic Places. <http://www.nationalregisterofhistoricplaces.com/TX/Brewster/state.html> [Accessed Mar 7 16:36:00 US/Central 2006].

49. "Wax, men, and money: candelilla wax camps along the Rio Grande." Texas Beyond History. <http://www.texasbeyondhistory.net/waxcamps/> [Accessed Apr 1 10:26:00 US/Central 2006].

50. "Chavarria". Heritage Quest Online. ProQuest Information and Learning Company. <http://www.heritagequestonline.com/> [Accessed Mar 27 07:25:00 US/Central 2006].

52. "Payne". Heritage Quest Online. ProQuest Information and Learning Company. <http://www.heritagequestonline.com/> [Mar 8, 2006].

53. "Rice". Heritage Quest Online. ProQuest Information and Learning Company. <http://www.heritagequestonline.com/> [Accessed Mar 8 07:38:00 US/Central 2006].

54. "Sublett". Heritage Quest Online. ProQuest Information and Learning Company. <http://www.heritagequestonline.com/> [Accessed Mar 9 12:51:00 US/Central 2006].

56. Flippin, Jack. "In search of the bend. Mariscal Canyon is where the Rio Grande makes its sweeping turn, but getting there and back is no easy trip." Houston Chronicle, Sunday, 06/27/1993. Section: Texas Magazine, Page 8, 2 Star Edition.

59. "San Vicente, Texas." The Handbook of Texas Online. <http://www.tsha.utexas.edu/handbook/online/articles/SS/hvs23.html> [Accessed Mar 23 08:42:00 US/Central 2000].

62. "Mercury mining." The Handbook of Texas Online. <http://www.tsha.utexas.edu/handbook/online/articles/MM/dkm2.html> [Accessed Oct 29 10:19:01 US/Central 2002].

63. "Terlingua, Texas." The Handbook of Texas Online. <http://www.tsha.utexas.edu/handbook/online/articles/TT/hnt13.html> [Accessed Oct 19 10:15:01 US/Central 2002].

65. "Smithers, Wilfred Dudley." The Handbook of Texas Online. <http://www.tsha.utexas.edu/handbook/online/articles/SS/fsm78.html> [Accessed Oct 29 10:29:00 US/Central 2002].

66. "Blue Creek." The Handbook of Texas Online. <http://www.tsha.utexas.edu/handbook/online/articles/BB/rbbfh.html> [Oct 29, 2002].

67. "G4 Ranch." The Handbook of Texas Online. <http://www.tsha.utexas.edu/handbook/online/articles/GG/apg4.html> [Accessed Oct 29 10:24:00   US/Central 2002].

68. "Castolon, Texas." The Handbook of Texas Online. <http://www.tsha.utexas.edu/handbook/online/articles/CC/hrc31.html> [Accessed Mar 19 16:43:01 US/Central 2006].

70. "San Vicente, Texas." The Handbook of Texas Online. <http://www.tsha.utexas.edu/handbook/online/articles/SS/hvs23.html> [Accessed Mar 1 07:32:01 US/Central 2006].

71. "Camp Neville Springs." The Handbook of Texas Online. <http://www.tsha.utexas.edu/handbook/online/> [Accessed March 22, 2000].

72. "River trip camping advisory." Big Bend National Park. National Park Service. <http://www.nps.gov/bibe/backcountry/river-camping.htm> [Accessed Mar 7 11:30:00 US/Central 2006].

73. "Castolon Historic District." Big Bend National Park. National Park Service. <http://www.nps.gov/bibe/castolon.htm> [Accessed Mar 22 13:24:00 US/Central 2000].

74. "Village of Boquillas, Mexico." Big Bend National Park. National Park Service. <http://www.nps.gov/bibe/boquillas.htm> [Accessed Mar 22 13:16:00 US/Central 2000].

75. "Village of Santa Elena, Mexico." Big Bend National Park. National Park Service. <http://www.nps.gov/bibe/boquillas.htm> [Accessed Mar 22 13:18:00 US/Central 2000].

77. "Cultural history of Big Bend National Park." Big Bend National Park. National Park Service. <http://www.nps.gov/bibe/CR/history.htm> [Accessed Mar 6 16:32:00 US/Central 2006].

78. "Hot Springs Historic District." Big Bend National Park. National Park Service. <http://www.nps.gov/bibe/CR/hotsp.htm> [Accessed Mar 6 16:32:00 US/Central 2006].

80. "Glenn Springs." Big Bend National Park. National Park Service. <http://www.nps.gov/bibe/CR/glennsp.htm> [Accessed Mar 6 16:29:00 US/Central 2006].

81. "Johnsons Ranch, the Air Corps in Big Bend." Big Bend National Park. National Park Service. <http://www.nps.gov/bibe/CR/jranch.htm> [Accessed Mar 6 16:28:00 US/Central 2006].

82. "Mariscal Mine." Big Bend National Park. National Park Service. <http://www.nps.gov/bibe/CR/mariscal.htm> [Acc'd Mar 6, 2006].

83. "La Harmonia Company store, Castolon." Big Bend National Park. National Park Service. <http://www.nps.gov/bibe/CR/lhstore.htm> [Accessed Mar 6 16:26:00 US/Central 2006].

84. "Babb". Heritage Quest Online. ProQuest Information and Learning Company. <http://www.heritagequestonline.com/> [Apr 4 2006].

85. Morin, Richard. Personal communication, February 3, 2006.

86. "Big Bend Geneological Society." Rootsweb.com <http://www.rootsweb.com/~txbcgs/r.html> [Accessed April 1, 2006].

87. "Foley, Washington Greenlee." The Handbook of Texas Online. <http://www.tsha.utexas.edu/handbook/online/articles/FF/ffo36.html> [Accessed Apr 9 10:36:01 US/Central 2006].

88. "Buchel County." The Handbook of Texas Online. <http://www.tsha.utexas.edu/handbook/online/articles/BB/hcb71.html> [Accessed Apr 9 10:31:00 US/Central 2006].

89. "Buchel, Augustus Carl." The Handbook of Texas Online. <http://www.tsha.utexas.edu/handbook/online/articles/BB/fbu3_print.html> [Accessed Apr 9 10:34:00 US/Central 2006].

90. "1895 U. S. Atlas." CFC Productions. <http://www.livgenmi.com/1895/TX/County/foley.htm> [Accessed April 9, 2006].

91. "Foley County." The Handbook of Texas Online. <http://www.tsha.utexas.edu/handbook/online/articles/FF/hcf71.html> [Accessed Apr 9 10:24:00 US/Central 2006].

92. "Brewster County, Texas. Marks & Brands." Rootsweb.com <http://www.rootsweb.com/~txbews2/marksbrands.html> [Accessed Apr 1 14:17:00 US/Central 2006].

93. "Rooney". Heritage Quest Online. ProQuest Information and Learning Company. <http://www.heritagequestonline.com/> [Accessed Apr 4 14:23:00 US/Central 2006].

95. "Pettit". Heritage Quest Online. ProQuest Information and Learning Company. <http://www.heritagequestonline.com/> [Apr 4, 2006].

101. Drijvers, Jan Willem. "Helena Augusta (248/249-328/329 A.D.)." De Imperatoribus Romanis. <http://www.roman-emperors.org/helena.htm> [Accessed Apr 22 07:28:00 US/Central 2006].

104. "Brewster County Geneological Society." Rootsweb.com <http://www.rootsweb.com/~txbrews/queries98.htm> [Acc'd Apr 1 l, 2006].

105. "Coahuila." Maps of Mexico. <http://www.maps-of-mexico.com/chihuahua-state-mexico/chihuahua-state-mexico-map-main.shtml> [Accessed Apr 1 15:58:00 US/Central 2006].

106. Langford, J. Oscar. Big Bend, a homesteaders story. Austin: University of Texas Press, 1973.

107. Ewald, Stanley. My name is Frederick Rice and I was born here. Houston: Nellie Rice, 1995.

109. "Hatch, E. H.". Heritage Quest Online. ProQuest Information and Learning Company. <http://www.heritagequestonline.com/> [Accessed Apr 28 10:50:00 US/Central 2006].

110. "Rutledge / Solis.". Heritage Quest Online. ProQuest Information and Learning Company. <http://www.heritagequestonline.com/> [Accessed Apr 28 10:58:00 US/Central 2006].

112. "Rio Grande Village, self-guiding nature trail, Big Bend National Park." Big Bend Natural History Association, 1989.

113. "Castolon." Big Bend Natural History Association, [1978?]

114. Novovitch, Barbara. "Efforts to Save Bridge to La Linda Accelerate." The Marathon Gazette, Vol. 1, February, 2002. Marathon, TX.

115. "Heath". Heritage Quest Online. ProQuest Information and Learning Company. <http://www.heritagequestonline.com/> [Accessed Apr 29 13:09:00 US/Central 2006].

117. Echols, Lt. William H. "Report in United States. Thirty-sixth Congress, Second Session, Senate Execute Document, No. 1 (Washington, 1861), 37-50." Ron's Texas Page. <http://www.qsl.net/w5www/texas.htm> [Accessed April 29, 2006].

118. Big Bend National Park Project. United States. Department of the Interior. National Park Service. [1964?]

120. Tyler, Ronnie C. The Big Bend: a history of the last Texas frontier. Washington: US GPO, 1975. Pgs. 10, 11, 13, 14, 64, 65, 67, 78, 82, 89, 91, 120, 121, 127, 133, 139, 147, 150, 154, 155, 163, 167, 213, 220, 221.

123. Yates, John P. "Tracing the Comanche War Trail." Presented at the Houston Archeological Society Meeting, May 12, 2006.

124. Wunderlich, Bonnie. "The Name Terlingua." Terlingua City Limits. <http://www.terlinguacitylimits.com/terlinguatpostoff> [Accessed May 12 18:48:00 US/Central 2006].

125. "Historic Big Bend and Terlingua Maps, 1822-1961." Terlingua Gallery. <http://www.terlinguagallery.com/terlinguadistrictsuvery> [Accessed May 14 10:15:00 US/Central 2006].

128. "Statement of Frank Deckert, Superintendent, Big Bend National Park...before the House Government Reform Subcommittee...April 15, 2003." National Park Service. <http://www.nps.gov/legal/testimony/108th/lebigben.htm> [Accessed May 20, 2006.]

129. "Brewster County." The Handbook of Texas Online. <http://www.tsha.utexas.edu/handbook/online/articles/BB/hcb14.html> [Accessed May 20 20:47:00 US/Central 2006].

130. "Brewster, Henry Percy." The Handbook of Texas Online. <http://www.tsha.utexas.edu/handbook/online/articles/BB/fbr44.html> [Accessed May 21 08:21:00 US/Central 2006].

131. "Graddy". Heritage Quest Online. ProQuest Information and Learning Company. <http://www.heritagequestonline.com/> [Accessed May 21 10:13:00 US/Central 2006].

132. "Williams". Heritage Quest Online. ProQuest Information and Learning Company. <http://www.heritagequestonline.com/> [Accessed May 21 10:30:00 US/Central 2006].

133. "Glasscock". Heritage Quest Online. ProQuest Information and Learning Company. <http://www.heritagequestonline.com/> [Accessed May 21 16:48:00 US/Central 2006].

137. "Sierra Caballo Muerto." The Handbook of Texas Online. <http://www.tsha.utexas.edu/handbook/online/articles/SS/rjs81.html> [Accessed May 29 09:02:00 US/Central 2006].

138. Reeve, Frank D. "The Apache Indians in Texas." Vol 050 No 2, Southwestern Historical Quarterly Online. <http://www.tsha.utexas.edu/publications/journals/shq/online/v050/n2/contrib_DIVL3107.html> [Accessed July 4, 2006].

139. Mallouf, Robert J. "On the trail with Apache Adams." La Vista de la Frontera. Vol 16, Number 1 (Summer 2004). Alpine: Center for Big Bend Studies. Sul Ross University.

140. Wulfkuhle, Virginia A. The Buttrill Ranch complex, Brewster County, Texas: evidence of early ranching in the Big Bend. Austin: Texas Historical Commission, 1986.

143. "Boquillas, Texas." The Handbook of Texas Online. <http://www.tsha.utexas.edu/handbook/online/articles/BB/hvb82.html> [Accessed Jul 9 20:20:00 US/Central 2006].

145. "Mineral resources and mining." The Handbook of Texas Online. <http://www.tsha.utexas.edu/handbook/online/articles/MM/gpm1.html> [Accessed Jul 15 05:22:00 US/Central 2006].

146. "Lindsey". Heritage Quest Online. ProQuest Information and Learning Company. <http://www.heritagequestonline.com/> [Accessed Jul 15 07:34:00 US/Central 2006].

149. "Moser". Heritage Quest Online. ProQuest Information and Learning Company. <http://www.heritagequestonline.com/> [Accessed Jul 15 20:24:00 US/Central 2006].

150. "Hernandez". Heritage Quest Online. ProQuest Information and Learning Company. <http://www.heritagequestonline.com/> [Accessed Jul 23 17:13:00 US/Central 2006].

151. "Steele". Heritage Quest Online. ProQuest Information and Learning Company. <http://www.heritagequestonline.com/> [Accessed Jul 23 19:46:00 US/Central 2006].

152. "Metcalf." Heritage Quest Online. ProQuest Information and Learning Company. <http://www.heritagequestonline.com/

Index

Biographical Note

Louis F. Aulbach

Author and Publisher of Texas River Guides

Louis Aulbach publishes maps and guidebooks for the wild West Texas rivers.

He has co-authored river guides for the Rio Grande Wild and Scenic River, including *The Lower Canyons of the Rio Grande*, the authoritative guide for the Lower Canyons, and *The Upper Canyons of the Rio Grande*, a guide that covers the magnificent Santa Elena Canyon. The *Lower Pecos River* is a guide to a well-hidden gem of a wilderness river that is a tributary of the Rio Grande. *The Devils River* provides information about this unique West Texas river, also a tributary of the Rio Grande.

The Great Unknown of the Rio Grande is a guide to the Rio Grande between Santa Elena Canyon and La Linda. It includes two spectacular canyons within Big Bend National Park, Mariscal Canyon and Boquillas Canyon.

Each book includes comprehensive discussions on what to take on a wilderness river trip, what to see and what to do, plus mile by mile topographical maps including campsites, rapids, canyons, fresh water springs and other natural features.

Louis Aulbach relaxes in camp after a good day of paddling on the Rio Grande.

Aulbach's most recent projects include *Buffalo Bayou, An Echo of Houston's Wilderness Beginnings*, and *Camp Logan, Houston, Texas, 1917-1919*. Both of these volumes delve into the local history of the city of Houston. A third publication, *The Fresno Rim*, is a hiking guide to the Big Bend Ranch State Park in West Texas.

All of his publications are available from your local retailer or from Amazon.com.

Aulbach, a native Houstonian, is a graduate of Rice University and the University of Chicago. He retired in 2008 after over seventeen years as the Records Management Officer for the City of Houston. He served on the Harris County Historical Commission in the 2009-2010 term.

He is an avid backpacker and canoeist who has traveled widely in the wilderness areas of Texas, Colorado, New Mexico, Wyoming and Alaska. He especially enjoys paddling the rivers of Texas with his daughter, Rachel, and his two sons, Stephen and Matthew, each of whom is an accomplished outdoorsman and canoeist in his own right. Each, too, has contributed illustrations and photographs to Aulbach's books.

(Continued from the back cover.)

household and had a big garden of vegetables and tomatoes. Son Thomas, born Oct 15, 1898 in Mexico, herded goats and later worked as a ranch hand. Son Rocky, born March 25, 1906, was a well known cowboy who worked throughout the Big Bend for many years[140]. The census of 1910 confirms that Monroe Payne, 39, his wife Jesusita, 32, and three sons and three daughters were living on the ranch of 43 year old rancher Lucius F. Buttrill[52].

In 1916, Monroe Payne was working as a supply clerk at the trading post at Boquillas, Texas (near today's Rio Grande Village) owned by Jesse Deemer[107]. On May 5, 1916, the same night that bandits attacked Glenn Springs, a separate group raided the Deemer store. Deemer and his supply clerk Monroe Payne were taken hostage and held in Mexico for three days[1].

Joe H. Graham bought the Buttrill Ranch from Lucius Buttrill in 1917, but by this time, Payne had acquired some land at Bone Springs. Bone Springs, known as Guaronza Spring or Guavanga Spring on 19th and early 20th century maps, got its name from the animal bones lying around the site of the spring. The seeps of the spring made a boggy area of soft mud around the spring and many animals who approached the spring for a drink got stuck in the mud and died[140]. The water of Bone Spring has a high alkaline content as indicated by the white residue around area of the spring[140], but, as Frederick Rice has commented, it was "wet[107]."

Payne and his family lived at Bone Springs for many years. He worked for Joe Graham periodically, sometimes as a cook, and in 1920, Monroe, 48, worked as a ranch laborer, as did his son Thomas. His daughter Maria, 24, was employed as a servant to a private family while his wife and four other children maintained the household[52].

Later, Payne sold a section of land near Bone Springs to Frederick Rice, Sr. and they moved to Marathon where they lived in a large house. By 1930, Payne, his wife, and three grown sons were living in Marathon's "East Mexico" neighborhood[52]. The aging Monroe Payne diversified into numerous business ventures including hauling supplies, renting property, bootlegging and selling water from his well[45].

Today, the story of the Black Seminoles in the Big Bend is a distant memory, and as time goes by, the story is fading fast. The only tangible reminders of this part of the history of the Big Bend are the fragile ruins at Neville Springs which include two structures. The most prominent of these is the officers quarters, a two room stone house approximately 18 feet by 36 feet in size. About 600 yards away, and closer to the spring, is the foundation of the enlisted men's barracks. This 20 foot by 60 foot two room building included the living area and a small blacksmith shop on the east end. A corral area is nearby[107].

A solitary grave rests on the site. After the camp was deactivated, settlers to the Big Bend lived near the spring at various times. Rosalie Juarez died on January 31, 1896, and she is buried in the lone grave[107]. Around the turn of the twentieth century, John Rice and his wife Ida stayed at Neville Springs for a short time while they were looking for a place to build a house and a ranch, which they finally did at Chilicotol Spring. John Rice claimed that there were five Black Seminoles buried there at Camp Neville Springs[107], too, but no evidence as yet can confirm that. It is a place of tenuous history.

The house at Bone Springs stands near the spring.

Photo Credit: Louis F. Aulbach

Made in the USA
Columbia, SC
25 March 2025

55659029R00064